Folklore from Africa to the United States

Folklore from Africa

to the United States

AN ANNOTATED BIBLIOGRAPHY

Compiled by
MARGARET N. COUGHLAN
Children's Book Section
General Reference and Bibliography Division

LIBRARY OF CONGRESS • WASHINGTON • 1976

Illustrations on the title page: fox and baboon by Christine Price, from Singing Tales of Africa *by Adjai Robinson, item 61; rabbit from* The Ox of the Wonderful Horns, and Other African Folktales *by Ashley Bryan, item 14. The turtle at the beginning of each chapter is also from* The Ox of the Wonderful Horns.

Library of Congress Cataloging in Publication Data

Coughlan, Margaret N 1925–
   Folklore from Africa to the United States.

   Includes index.
   1. Folk-lore, Negro—Bibliography—Catalogs.
   2. Folk-lore—Africa—Bibliography—Catalogs.
   3. Folk-lore—West Indies—Bibliography—Catalogs.
   4. Folk-lore—United States—Bibliography—Catalogs.
   5. United States, Library of Congress. I. Title.
Z5984.A35C68 [GR350]   016.398   75–43905
ISBN 0–8444–0175–7

For sale by the Superintendent of Documents, U.S. Government Printing Office
Washington, D.C. 20402 - Price: $4.50
Stock Number: 030–001–00066–4

Foreword

In the body of American folklore, which is both indigenous and related to that of other lands, one portion is identified as having come to this country from the African continent. Richard A. Waterman and William R. Bascom point out in "African and New World Negro Folklore" (item 180) that "surviving the drastic social changes that accompanied the forceful transplanting of African peoples into slavery on a strange continent, . . . Negro folklore has persisted in the New World as a well-defined and basically homogeneous entity."

The narrative, along with the riddle, proverb, song, or game, has been dominant in Negro oral literature. Some of these black (or Afro-American) tales have become as much a part of the heritage of American children as has classic folklore derived from European sources. Most popular among them have been the animal tales revolving about Brer Rabbit and his companions.

In the latter half of the 19th century a paternalistic interest was shown by missionaries to Africa—and soon after by civil servants, linguists, and ethnologists—in recording African tales in their many original languages and then translating them into English, French, German, and other languages of the colonial powers. The intent was to preserve the tales "in the name of progress and civilization" (see item 105) and to enable study that would promote an understanding of the peoples by the white man and also provide textbook reading matter in African languages for use by non-African government workers as well as by Africans. It is recognized, however, that there is no complete collection of mythical tales representing any one of the thousands of African peoples. Preservation was also a motive of collectors in the West Indies and the United States.

The purpose of this bibliography is to reveal original sources of African tales and to trace their relationship to stories carried to the West Indies and the American South, including the Sea Islands, South Carolina, where the tales were told in the Gullah patois. These stories were chiefly animal and trickster tales. But as it developed, black American folklore was to include not only these tales, clearly related to Africa, but also tall stories and others which came to be told about black American folk heroes, like John Henry, Daddy Mention, and the slave John.

The following entries, composing a selective rather than a comprehensive bibliography, describe works available in the collections of the Library of Congress. For the most part, they cite collections of folklore, but a few linguistic, ethnological, and anthropological studies and some travel accounts and government reports containing tales are also included. The titles were selected because they shed light on the cultures out of which the tales arose and are fruitful sources for retellings for children. The geographical arrangement brings items together in four major African land areas—West, South, Central, and East—preceded by an opening section on general works and followed by sections on the West Indies and the United States. The bibliography is limited to English-language works except for a few French-language items for Africa and the West Indies.

Criteria for inclusion of collections for children are the citation of printed sources where possible, faithful treatment of cultural backgrounds, and a style approximating the original in directness and simplicity, if not in starkness. In some instances the annotations indicate inappropriate style and distorted adaptation, such as the deliberate softening of incident and characterization to make a story palatable to other cultures. Single-tale picture books are excluded as main entries but in a few cases have been cited in notes for longer works.

Call numbers indicate location of the items in the Library of Congress collections. "Micro" is the designation for location in the Microform Reading Room.

The Children's Book Section acknowledges with gratitude the assistance of specialists in the African Section for the identification of proper forms of names of peoples and geographical areas.

Virginia Haviland
Head, Children's Book Section

Contents

Foreword — v

Acknowledgments — viii

SUB-SAHARAN AFRICA — 1
- Studies and Bibliographies — 1
- Collections for Adults — 7
- Collections for Children — 8

WEST AFRICA — 13
- Studies and Collections for Adults — 13
- Collections for Children — 35

SOUTHERN AFRICA — 51
- Studies and Collections for Adults — 51
- Collections for Children — 63

CENTRAL AFRICA — 69
- Studies and Collections for Adults — 69
- Collections for Children — 75

EAST AFRICA — 81
- Studies and Collections for Adults — 81
- Collections for Children — 92

THE WEST INDIES — 103
- Studies and Collections for Adults — 103
- Collections for Children — 115

THE UNITED STATES — 123
- Studies and Collections for Adults — 124
- Collections for Children — 146

Index — 153

Acknowledgments

Illustrations on the title page: the fox and the baboon are by Christine Price, from *Singing Tales of Africa* by Adjai Robinson, text copyright © 1974 Adjai Robinson, illustrations copyright © 1974 Christine Price, used by permission of Charles Scribner's Sons; the rabbit as well as the turtle which appears at the beginning of each chapter are from *The Ox of the Wonderful Horns, and Other African Folktales* by Ashley Bryan, copyright © 1971 by Ashley Bryan, used by permission of Atheneum Publishers.

The illustration on page xii by Grisha Dotzenko, from *African Folk Tales* by Charlotte and Wolf Leslau, copyright © 1963 by the Peter Pauper Press, is reproduced by permission of Peter Pauper Press.

The illustration on page 6 by Kate Marr, from *African Genesis* by Leo Frobenius and Douglas C. Fox, copyright 1937 by Leo Frobenius and Douglas C. Fox, is reproduced by permission of Stackpole Books.

The illustration on page 9 is from *The Ox of the Wonderful Horns, and Other African Folktales* by Ashley Bryan, copyright © 1971 by Ashley Bryan and used by permission of Atheneum Publishers.

The illustration on page 15 by Larry Lurin, from *Tales of Yoruba Gods and Heroes* by Harold Courlander, © 1973 by Harold Courlander, is used by permission of Crown Publishers, Inc.

The illustrations on pages 21 and 35 by Ib Ohlsson, from *Tales for the Third Ear, From Equatorial Africa* by Verna Aardema, text copyright © 1969 by Verna Aardema, illustrations copyright © 1969 by Ib Ohlsson, and that on page 97 by Christine Price, from *The Rich Man and the Singer; Folktales from Ethiopia* by Mesfin Habte-Mariam, edited and copyright © 1971 by Christine Price, are used by permission of E. P. Dutton & Co., Inc.

The illustrations on pages 24–25 and 44 from *Tales of Mogho;*

African Stories From Upper Volta by Frederic Guirma, copyright © 1971, Frederic Guirma, and that on page 43 from Guirma's *Princess of the Full Moon,* translated by John Garrett, copyright © 1970 Frederic Guirma and John Garrett, are used by permission of Macmillan Publishing Co., Inc.

The Hausa writing on page 30 from *Hausa Folk-Lore, Customs, Proverbs, Etc.*, vol. 1, by Robert Sutherland Rattray, is used by permission of The Clarendon Press, Oxford.

The illustration on page 32 by Ademola Olugebefola, from *Fourteen Hundred Cowries, and Other African Tales* collected by Abayomi Fuja, text copyright © 1962 by Oxford University Press, illustrations copyright © 1971 by Ademola Olugebefola, is used by permission of Lothrop, Lee & Shepard Company.

The illustration on page 36 by Gregorio Prestopino, from *Sundiata: The Epic of the Lion King* by Roland Bertol, copyright © 1970 by Roland Bertol, illustrations copyright © 1970 by Gregorio Prestopino; those on pages 98 and 99 by Leo and Diane Dillon, from W. Moses Serwadda's *Songs and Stories From Uganda,* transcribed and edited by Hewitt Pantaleoni, copyright © 1974 by W. Moses Serwadda and Hewitt Pantaleoni, illustrations copyright © 1974 by Leo and Diane Dillon; and that on page 114 by Marcia Brown, from *Anansi, the Spider Man; Jamaican Folk Tales* by Philip M. Sherlock, copyright 1954 by Philip M. Sherlock, are all used by permission of Thomas Y. Crowell Company, Inc.

The woodcut on page 49 by Helen Siegl, from *The Dancing Palm Tree, and Other Nigerian Folktales* by Barbara Walker, text copyright © 1968 by Barbara Walker, illustrations copyright © 1968 by Helen Siegl, is used by permission of Parents' Magazine Press.

The illustrations on pages 50, 62, and 63 by Leo and Diane Dillon, from *Behind the Back of the Mountain; Black Folktales From Southern Africa,* by Verna Aardema, text copyright © 1973 by Verna Aardema, pictures copyright © 1973 by Leo and Diane Dillon, and that on page 149 by Ralph Pinto, from *The Knee-High Man, and Other Tales* by Julius Lester, text copyright © 1972 by Julius Lester, illustrations copyright © 1972 by Ralph Pinto, are used by permission of The Dial Press.

The illustrations on pages 66 and 68 by Eric Byrd, from *The Lion on the Path, and Other African Stories* by Hugh Tracey, © Hugh Tracey 1967, are used by permission of Praeger Publishers and Routledge & Kegan Paul Ltd.

The woodcuts on pages 75 and 77 by Rocco Negri, from Virginia Holladay's *Bantu Tales*, edited by Louise Crane, text copyright © 1970 by Joseph C. Edens, Jr., illustrations copyright © 1970 by The Viking Press, Inc., and the illustration on page 94 by George Ford, from *Tales Told Near a Crocodile; Stories From Nyanza* by Humphrey Harman, copyright © 1962 by Humphrey Harman, are reprinted by permission of The Viking Press, Inc.

The illustration on page 80 by Robert W. Kane, from *The Fire on the Mountain, and Other Ethiopian Stories* by Harold Courlander and Wolf Leslau, copyright, 1950, by Henry Holt and Company, Inc., is reproduced by permission of Holt, Rinehart and Winston, Publishers.

The illustration on page 102 by Joan Kiddell-Monroe, from *West Indian Folk-Tales* by Philip Sherlock, © Philip Sherlock 1966, is used by permission of Oxford University Press.

The illustration on pages 116–17 by Trina Schart Hyman, from *Greedy Mariani and Other Folktales of the Antilles* by Dorothy Sharp Carter, copyright © 1974 by Dorothy Sharp Carter, illustrations copyright © 1974 by Atheneum Publishers, is used by permission of Atheneum Publishers. A Margaret K. McElderry Book.

The illustration on page 119 by Lucy Herndon Crockett, from *Uncle Bouqui of Haiti* by Harold Courlander, copyright 1942 by Harold Courlander, is used by permission of the author.

The illustrations on pages 122, 131, 132, 142, and 148 by Arthur Burdette Frost, from *The Complete Tales of Uncle Remus* by Joel Chandler Harris, compiled by Richard Chase, copyright © 1955 by Houghton Mifflin Company, are used by permission of Houghton Mifflin Company.

The illustration on page 145 by James Daugherty, from *John Henry and the Double Jointed Steam-Drill* by Irwin Shapiro, is reprinted by permission of Julian Messner, a Division of Simon & Schuster, Inc. Copyright 1945 by Irwin Shapiro.

The illustration on page 152 by Peggy Wilson, from *Ananse the Spider: Tales from an Ashanti Village* by Peggy Appiah, © copyright, 1966, by Peggy Appiah, is used by permission of Pantheon Books.

Sub-Saharan Africa

Entries in this section offer an overall view of the oral tradition from Africa south of the Sahara. Studies survey the collecting of tales and other oral literature, storytelling and stylistic devices, and criteria for evaluating books of African folklore for children. From English-language sources it is apparent that there has been increasing activity in the collecting and publishing of folklore for adults and children.

The anthologies present examples of genres of folklore gathered from many sources. Folklore journals, such as the *Journal of American Folklore* (v. 1+ April–June 1888+ Philadelphia, American Folklore Society, GR1.A5) and *Folk-Lore; a Quarterly Review* (v. 1+ March 1890+ London, Folk-Lore Society, GR1.F5), and other African-oriented periodicals have not been analyzed for this bibliography. These and other journals are listed in *Littérature orale Afrique noire; bibliographie analytique* (item 4). African specialists have compiled two of the bibliographies listed, one American, the other French. Both cite works directed to children.

STUDIES AND BIBLIOGRAPHIES

1. Dorson, Richard M., *comp.*
   AFRICAN FOLKLORE. Bloomington, Indiana University Press
   [1972] 587 p.   GR350.D67 1972b

   Includes bibliographical references.

   Papers presented by African and non-African folklorists, anthropologists, and oral literature and linguistic specialists at the Conference on African Folklore, Indiana University, July 16–18, 1970. The volume is divided into three parts: (1) "Africa and the Folklorist," an essay in which the compiler,

From *African Folk Tales* by *Charlotte and Wolf Leslau, illustrated by Grisha Dotzenko. Item 12.*

Distinguished Professor of History and Folklore and director of the Folklore Institute at Indiana University, discusses the relationship of folklore to oral literature, anthropology, and oral history; (2) papers by other scholars, arranged in the following categories: Traditional Narrative; Traditional Verbal Genres; Folklore and Literature; Tradition and History; Traditional Poetry; and Traditional Ritual; and (3) texts of tales recorded in the Sudan, Liberia, Ghana, Mali, Cameroon, Gabon, and South Africa.

Topics treated in depth include literary art, stylistic devices, the contrast between the traditional and the innovative storyteller, and such genres as the dilemma tale, which gives the listener "a choice between alternatives, such as which of several characters deserves a reward," the epic, and the heroic song.

The rich selection in part 3 of examples of prose and verse narrative indicates the abundant variety of folklore in African culture.

2. ———
THE BRITISH FOLKLORISTS; A HISTORY. [Chicago] University of Chicago Press [1968] 518 p. illus., ports.   GR50.D63

Bibliography: p. 442–460.

An informal history, with some analysis, of the development of the study of folklore in Great Britain and of those behind it. Pages 349–371 of chapter 10, "The Overseas Folklorists," concern Africa. Among the pioneers and specialists singled out for lengthy comment are Dr. Wilhelm Heinrich Immanuel Bleek, a German philologist who worked with Khoisan materials; the Reverend Canon Callaway, an English medical missionary and first Bishop of Kaffraria, who was concerned with the Zulu; George McCall Theal, who worked with the Xhosa; and Maj. Arthur John Newman Tremearne, who studied the Hausa.

3. Görög-Karady, Veronika.
[LITTÉRATURE ORALE DE L'AFRIQUE NOIRE; BIBLIOGRAPHIE ANALYTIQUE] Cahiers d'études africaines, v. 8, 3. cahier, 1968: 453–501; v. 9, 4. cahier, 1969: 641–666; v. 10, 4. cahier, 1970: 583–631; v. 12, 1. cahier, 1972: 174–192.
            DT1.C3, v. 8–10, 12

Part 1 cites general studies, bibliographies of oral literature, and "methodological" works (for example, Antti Aarne's *The Types of Folktale; a Classification and Bibliography* and Stith Thompson's *Motif-Index of Folk-Literature*) selected and annotated by a French scholar to indicate the most important studies in the field of oral literature and other significant though less familiar volumes. Part 1 also lists a number of editions for children, among them Kathleen Arnott's *African Myths and Legends* (see item 13), Eleanor B. Heady's *Jambo, Sungura! Tales From East Africa* (see item 125), and Harold Courlander's *The King's Drum, and Other African Stories* (see item 16).

Parts 2–4 consist of annotated references to texts, studies, and articles from international scholarly periodicals in the disciplines of folklore and ethnography. Among the sources of English-language entries are the *Journal of American Folklore* and *African Studies*.

Each of the four parts contains an ethnolinguistic index; part 4 also provides a tale type index.

An introduction was published in v. 8, 2. cahier, 1968, p. 310–317.

4. Herman, Gertrude B.
AFRICANA: FOLKLORE COLLECTIONS FOR CHILDREN. School library journal, v. 18, May 1972: 35–39.   Z671.L7, v. 18

Selected, annotated bibliography.

Among the criteria for books of African folklore for children discussed here are authenticity of sources, authority of the author, compiler, or collector, style, appeal for American children, and format. The author, an assistant professor at the Library School, University of Wisconsin, points out stylistic features and story elements encountered in African folklore and directs the reader to recognize the importance of cultural differences among African peoples.

5. Parrinder, Edward Geoffrey.
AFRICAN MYTHOLOGY. London, Hamlyn [1968, c1967] 139, [2] p. illus. (part col.), map.   BL2400.P34

Bibliography: p. [140]

In his introduction the author comments on the peoples of Africa and on their art—sculpture and painting—as a form of writing which interprets life and religion. Summarizing their oral narratives, he groups them into categories: The Creator,

God Leaves the World, The First Men, The Mystery of Birth, The Origins of Death, The World Beyond, Gods and Spirits, Oracles and Divination, Witches and Monsters, Secret Societies and Ancestors, Legends of Old Africa, and Animal Fables.

A primal myth from the Yoruba of Nigeria tells of Orisha Nla (Great God) who was sent by Ol-orun (Supreme Being) to create firm ground. Another, from the Fon of Dahomey, describes a snake which at the time of creation gathered the earth in its coils so that man could have a place to live. A Madagascar myth recounts how a man fell in love with a woman he carved out of wood. Hare and Spider tales are included in Animal Fables. Five Tar Baby stories are summarized here, two with Spider as the central figure and three with Hare.

6. Scheub, Harold.
BIBLIOGRAPHY OF AFRICAN ORAL NARRATIVES. Madison, African Studies Program, University of Wisconsin, 1971. 160 p. (University of Wisconsin. African Studies Program. Occasional paper no. 3)　　　　　　　　　　Z3508.L5S3

A multilingual finding list of adult and children's materials, which includes riddles and proverbs as well as stories. The compilation is divided into four parts—texts, a supplement to these, a Cultural-Linguistic Index, and bibliographies. Brief notations identify the contents of each numbered entry. Items for children are noted with asterisks.

7. Schmidt, Nancy J.
COLLECTIONS OF AFRICAN FOLKLORE FOR CHILDREN. Research in African literatures, v. 2, fall 1971: 150–167.　GR&B CBS

Extensive annotated bibliography.

A critical examination of collections of sub-Saharan African folklore published for children in the United States. The author, an anthropologist and African specialist, discusses criteria and such common failings in the tales as lack of African content, use of English equivalents for African proverbs, omission of African names, undocumented adaptation, and an overemphasis on animal tales, as well as the qualifications of the compiler-authors. Of particular value to reviewers, other writer-collectors of African folktales, and students is her appraisal of Hugh Tracey's *The Lion on the Path, and*

Other African Stories (item 90), a work she considers unique in that it is "truly African both in content and style."

8. Thompson, Stith.
THE FOLKTALE. New York, Dryden Press, 1946. 510 p.
PN1001.T5

A well-known authority's scholarly examination of the folk tale, its importance, history, and diffusion. Part two, European Asiatic Folktales in Other Continents, touches on African folklore with the author sketching its relationship to European, Asian, and Muslim cultures. He indicates an Indian origin for such popular figures as the Tar Baby and a European source for others like "The Theft of Butter (Honey) by Playing Godfather."

Appendix B contains a bibliography of African folklore studies (p. 471–472).

9. Werner, Alice.
MYTHS AND LEGENDS OF THE BANTU. [London] F. Cass, 1968. 334 p. illus., map, plates. (Cass library of African studies. General studies, no. 65) GR360.B2W4 1968

Reprint of 1933 ed.

Bibliography: p. 323–326.

A study of the oral literature of the "Bantu," which includes summaries of tales and only a few in their entirety. In her introduction the author describes Bantu-speaking peoples, their language, customs, and beliefs in a spirit world. Subjects examined in some detail include the beginnings of man, the coming of death, tricksters (Hlakanyana and Huveane), heroes, monsters, "Brer Rabbit in Africa," and other animal stories and legends.

"Brer Rabbit in Africa" and "Legends of the Tortoise" relate the Uncle Remus stories to their African ancestors. The scholar states, "On the one hand, every story in 'Uncle Remus' can be shown to exist in a more primitive shape in Africa, and among people who cannot be suspected of having imported it from America or elsewhere." She points out that though Negro slaves are supposed to have come from Bantu-speaking peoples in the Congo basin, "there is evidence that slaves were frequently, during the first quarter of the nineteenth century, imported from Mozambique and other ports on the East Coast. . . . This perhaps explains why the African

From African Genesis *by Leo Frobenius and Douglas C. Fox, illustrated by Kate Marr. Item 11.*

hare (Kalulu, of the Nyanja; Sungura, of the Swahili) should be such a prominent figure in Negro folklore, while his place is taken on the Congo (where it appears there are no hares) by the little antelope known as the water chevrotain. The slaves of the British West Indies were chiefly West Africans (Yorubas, Ibos, Fantis, etc.), and their 'Nancy' stories are mostly concerned with the spider (Anansi)."

In "African Mythology," which appears in volume 7 of *The Mythology of All Races* (New York, Cooper Square Publishers, 1964 [c1925] BL25.M8), the author provides an overview of the folklore and mythology of sub-Saharan Africa in which she gives scant attention to Arabic and European influences. The work includes summaries of many narratives. Chapter 6, "Heroes," chapter 11, "Hare and Jackal Stories," chapter 12, "Tortoise Stories," and chapter 13, "Spider Stories," discuss the roles and characteristics of the animal heroes, provide résumés of many tales, and comment on the relationship between the African ones and those of Brer Rabbit.

Extensive notes accompany each chapter.

COLLECTIONS FOR ADULTS

10. Cendrars, Blaise, *comp.*
    THE AFRICAN SAGA. Translated from L'Anthologie nègre by Margery Bianco. With an introduction by Arthur B. Spingarn. New York, Negro Universities Press [1969] 378 p.   GR350.C42 1969

Reprint of the 1927 ed.

Bibliography: p. 371–378.

One hundred and eight narratives, poems, and proverbs representing the genius of a people are translated from the poetic French of a Swiss-French poet and novelist. The compiler states that he has "given these tales [selected from published sources] just as the missionaries and explorers brought them to Europe. . . . They are not always the most original versions nor the most faithful translations . . . [since] literary exactitude was not the only legitimate preoccupation of these distant travellers."

The contents are varied. Creation stories include one of Nzame and "the beginning of everything." There are tales of supernatural creatures, cannibals, a man-eating rock, and talismans, like the yboumbouni's tail ("strong enough to carry a hundred elephants"). Among wonders recounted is the boy with the mark of a full moon on his chest; among legendary heroes is Ngurangurane, son of the crocodile.

11. Frobenius, Leo, *and* Douglas C. Fox.
    AFRICAN GENESIS. New York, Stackpole Sons [c1937] 236 p. illus., plates.   GR350.F74

The stories in the first two parts of this book have appeared in the Atlantis series of *Volksmärchen und Volksdichtungen Afrikas,* by Leo Frobenius, published 1921–24. The stories in the third part appeared in Frobenius' *Erythräa,* published in 1931.

Contents: The Berbers.—The Sudanese.—Southern Rhodesians.

Douglas Fox in his introduction comments on the different peoples, noting for the Kabyl of North Africa a relationship between the myths and rock pictures in the Sahara Atlas. He mentions further the culture of a heroic period as reflected in songs from the fourth to the 12th centuries and revealed in the Soninke epic the *Dausi.*

Among the 29 tales set down here are sources for *Gassire's Lute* (see Jablow's *Gassire's Lute,* item 59), "Kassa the Strong One," in Harold Courlander's *The Cow-Tail Switch* (item 51), and "The Talking Skull," in his *Terrapin's Pot of Sense* (item 185). Elements of the Jacob and Esau story appear in "The Rediscovery of Wagadu." The flavor of medieval romance permeates "Samba Gama."

A reprint of this classic work has been issued by B. Blom in New York (1966).

12. Leslau, Charlotte, *and* Wolf Leslau, eds.
    AFRICAN FOLK TALES. With decorations by Grisha Dotzenko. Mount Vernon, N.Y., Peter Pauper Press [c1963] 62 p. col. illus. PZ8.1.L43 Af

Twenty-five short, often gently didactic tales from the peoples of Africa represent stories of origins, how and why stories, and *Märchen* (fairytales). Among the latter are "The Marriage of the Mouse," reprinted from Harold Courlander's *Fire on the Mountain* (item 122), and "Hamdaani," a "Puss in Boots" variant found as "Sultan Darai" in Edward Steere's *Swahili Tales* (item 120) and as "Haamdaane" in George W. Bateman's *Zanzibar Tales* (item 120).

Strong, three-color linocuts decorate the small volume.

COLLECTIONS FOR CHILDREN

13. Arnott, Kathleen.
    AFRICAN MYTHS AND LEGENDS. Illustrated by Joan Kiddell-Monroe. New York, H. Z. Walck, 1963 [c1962] 211 p. (Oxford myths and legends) PZ8.1.A73 Af 2

Bibliography of sources.

The narratives in this volume, representing popular how and why stories and *Märchen* (fairytales), have been selected from the oral traditions of people south of the Sahara. Told in a conversational style, with explanatory details worked into the texts, they retain a few African names and songs, such as the following from "The Singing Drum and the Mysterious Pumpkin":

> I have left my shell,
> My beautiful shell,

Which shines like the moon,
On the bare, grey rock.

Among favorites here are "The Magic Drum," "Snake Magic," "The Tug of War," "The Monkey's Heart," "The Rubber Man" (a Tar Baby variant), and "The Magic Horns." There are also a few trickster tales, with Spider, Tortoise, and Hare rotating as heroes. Handsomely illustrated.

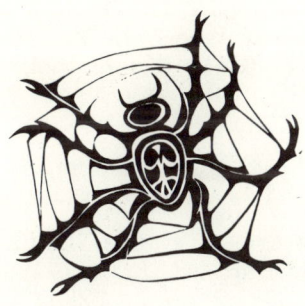

From The Ox of the Wonderful Horns, and Other African Folktales by Ashley Bryan. Item *14*.

14. Bryan, Ashley.
    THE OX OF THE WONDERFUL HORNS, AND OTHER AFRICAN FOLKTALES. Retold and illustrated by Ashley Bryan. New York, Atheneum, 1971. 42 p.   PZ8.1.B838 Ox

Contents: Ananse the spider in search of a fool.—Frog and his two wives.—Elephant and Frog go courting.—Tortoise, Hare, and the sweet potatoes.—The ox of the wonderful horns.

Five vigorous and entertaining stories from Angola, South Africa, and West Africa, strikingly illustrated with the author's woodcuts, some in three colors. The tellings are enriched by formula beginnings and endings such as "We do not mean, we do not really mean, that what we are going to say is true" and "Whether good, whether bad, there is nothing to add. I have finished." Sources for the stories are cited.

15. Carpenter, Frances.
    AFRICAN WONDER TALES. Illustrated by Joseph Escourido. Garden City, N.Y., Doubleday [1963] 215 p.
    PZ8.1.C227 Af

Culled by the author from French and English written sources, these 24 stories are presented formally, as if she were telling them directly to children. Her use of songs strengthens a sense of the original style, and her introduction of customs and other necessary explanatory material is unobtrusive.

One encounters marvels like the "Wonder Boy," who talked and walked at birth; the "boom-boom-y," a mighty beast of ancient times with a tail 10 times the size of a lion's and covered with white hairs so that it resembled "a trailing cloud in the sky"; and beasts who could change into men. Among favorite themes is that of a girl in a drum ("The Cannibal and His Singing Bird"), a girl concealed in the skin of a snake ("Polo, the Snake Girl"), and a magic drum capable of producing quantities of food ("The Tortoise and the Magic Drum"). "The Monkeys and the Little Red Hats" may be a source for Esphyr Slobodkina's picture book tale *Caps for Sale*.

Full-page line drawings depict lively action.

16. Courlander, Harold, *comp*.
 THE KING'S DRUM, AND OTHER AFRICAN STORIES. Illustrated by Enrico Arno. New York, Harcourt, Brace & World [1962] 125 p.   PZ8.1.C8 Ki

An assortment of tales gathered from the Bema, Bakongo, Mbako, Masai, Ashanti, Ewe, Hausa, and Mende peoples. They tell of tricksters, heroes (true and false), dilemmas, and conflicts. All have much to say about human nature. Some are humorous, some poignant, and some subtly philosophical, like "How Poverty Was Revealed to the King of Adja":

> Adjahosu, the King of Adja, had everything. One day he went to see his diviner. He said to him, "You must divine something for me. I am too rich and do not know what it is to be poor. I want to know what it is to be poor."
>
> The diviner took his divining shells; he threw them on the earth and studied them. Many times he tossed the shells and read their meaning. Then he told the King of Adja to bring him a drum, a gong, and rattles. He told the King of Adja to have his hunters catch a giraffe. . . .

Background material, sources, and comments on different versions appear in notes on the stories.

17. Savory, Phyllis, *comp*.
 LION OUTWITTED BY HARE, AND OTHER AFRICAN TALES. Illustrated by Franz Altschuler. Chicago, A. Whitman [1971] 160 p.   PZ8.1.S257 Li

Contents: Tales told by the Matabele people: How the lion

was outwitted by the hare. Why the hippopotamus left the forest. The hare's rope trick. The tortoise who dared the hare. How the bat made his choice.—Tales told in Malawi and Kenya: The bushbuck's visitor. The lion and the little brown bird. How a poor man was rewarded. The lazy son. The bird with the golden legs.—Tales told by the Zulu people: The tortoise and his boast. The song of the doves.—Tales told by the Xhosa people: The moon girl. The magic bowl and spoon. When the husband stayed home. The wonderful water pot. What the fish promised.

These 17 well-told and attractively presented tales come from Southern and Eastern Africa. Grouped by people or locale, they include animal stories and narratives of magic. They represent a judicious selection from five volumes of the author's out of print Fireside Tales Series (Cape Town, H. Timmins): *Basuto Fireside Tales,* illustrated by Jillian Hulme (1962. 64 p. GR360.B3S3); *Fireside Tales From the North,* illustrated by Jillian Hulme (1966. 86 p. GR360.K43S2); *Matabele Fireside Tales,* illustrated by Sylvia Baxter (1962. 75 p. GR360.M34S3); *Xhosa Fireside Tales,* illustrated by Gerard Bhengu (1963. 100 p. GR360.X6S3); and *Zulu Fireside Tales,* illustrated by Sylvia Baxter (New York, Hastings House [1961] 64 p. GR360.Z8S3).

Under the title *Bantu Folk Tales From Southern Africa* (Cape Town, H. Timmins [1974] 203 p. illus. GR360.B2S18), tales from eight of the "Bantu" peoples have also been selected from the Fireside Tales Series. Jillian Hulme's illustrations have been retained. A further volume in the series is *Bechuana Fireside Tales,* illustrated by Jillian Hulme (1965. 82 p. GR360.B2S19). Additional collections from the same publisher but not in the series are *Fireside Tales of the Hare and His Friends* (1965. GR360.B2S2) and *Swazi Fireside Tales* (1962. GR360.S85S28), both illustrated by Jillian Hulme. The first contains more animal stories from Southern and Eastern Africa; the other has fairytales from Southern Africa, seven of which—"Setuli," "The Cock's Kraal," "The Moss Green Princess," "The Cloud Princess," "The Bewitched Buck," "Tombe-Ende," and "The White Dove"—have been "reconstructed" from versions first appearing in *Fairy Tales From South Africa,* by Mrs. E. J. Bourhill and Mrs. J. B. Drake (item 85).

Throughout these collections appear stories with Scandinavian and Teutonic equivalents, like "The Husband Who Wanted To Mind the House" (here "When the Husband Stayed Home").

Except as noted, specific printed sources are not indicated.

18. Woodson, Carter G.
AFRICAN MYTHS, TOGETHER WITH PROVERBS; A SUPPLEMENTARY READER COMPOSED OF FOLK TALES FROM VARIOUS PARTS OF AFRICA, ADAPTED TO THE USE OF CHILDREN IN THE PUBLIC SCHOOLS. [2d ed.] Washington, Associated Publishers [c1948] xvii, 184 p. illus. PE1127.G4W7 1948

In his preface the scholar-author, describing the role and method of the storyteller, notes that the selections in this volume "are merely a few legends from different sources. . . . These are presented here without modification of thought but in the simplest language possible to reach the minds of children of the lower grades of public schools."

Mildly instructive are the appealing stories about the beginnings of things, tales of animals and everyday life in the bush, and "The Legend of Ngurangurane," a great magician who was the son of the crocodile. Together they reveal the evils of greed, jealousy, ingratitude, and other undesirable human traits. The inclusion of proverbs, chants and songs, and the names of people create a strong sense of authenticity.

West Africa

This area comprises Niger, Nigeria, Mali, Upper Volta, Dahomey, Togo, Ghana, Ivory Coast, Liberia, Sierra Leone, Guinea, Portuguese Guinea, Senegal, Gambia, and Mauritania.

A vast amount of folklore has been recorded in West Africa, where, however, there remain still untouched areas for the collector. The Hausa tales clearly reveal a Muslim influence, preserved both through oral transmission and in Arabic manuscripts. The Yoruba have a rich mythology, as is shown by Harold Courlander. The epic *Sundiata* is still part of oral literature in the western savanna region. The Ashanti have Anansi the Spider, while the Hausas tell about Spider, or Gizo, and Jackal and less often about the Hare, Zomo. The Yoruba have Ajapa the Tortoise, or "bald-headed elf."

STUDIES AND COLLECTIONS FOR ADULTS

19. Barker, William H., *and* Cecilia Sinclair.
    WEST AFRICAN FOLK-TALES. With frontispiece & 23 drawings by Cecilia Sinclair. New foreword by Hermese Roberts. Northbrook, Ill., Metro Books, 1972. 183 p.
    PZ8.1.B27 We

The author, formerly principal of a government teacher-training institution, collected these 36 Spider (Anansi) tales, how and why stories, and *Märchen* from its first students, mature men who had had experience in their district schools. In his introduction he describes a setting for village storytelling, discusses the European impact on Gold Coast peoples, and comments on the tales and their equivalents in other cultures. The stories are short, frequently didactic, with editorial interpolations pointing out Anansi's "wicked ways." Anansi is depicted as conniving, malevolent, and greedy, as in most of the Spider stories. Two stories have a tiger as central character. A footnote explains that in West Africa the tiger is a leopard.

20. Basden, George T.
NIGER IBOS; A DESCRIPTION OF THE PRIMITIVE LIFE, CUSTOMS AND ANIMISTIC BELIEFS, &C., OF THE IBO PEOPLE OF NIGERIA BY ONE WHO, FOR THIRTY-FIVE YEARS, ENJOYED THE PRIVILEGE OF THEIR INTIMATE CONFIDENCE AND FRIENDSHIP. With 70 illustrations and a sketch map and a new bibliographical note by John Ralph Willis. [2d ed.] New York, Barnes & Noble [1966] 456 p. DT515.B34 1966a

" . . . a fundamental study of many aspects of Ibo life and culture." In a bibliographical note to the 1966 edition, John Ralph Willis comments on the uniqueness of this work, a product of the missionary-author's long residency among the Ibo, when he became familiar with ancient customs and traditions ordinarily concealed from the stranger. His full bibliography (p. 440–445) has seven sections.

The author introduces sympathetically the plight of the Ibo at a time when "the balance of life [was] disturbed" by the gradual demise of "native law and custom" under British administration. He tells of the difficulties of acquiring reliable information on old beliefs and customs, stressing that "the substance of this book is concerned with the Ibo people as they *were*—not as they are at the present day."

Chapter 33, "Fireside Stories," supplies nine Ibo narratives and a number of proverbs. Four tales about Tortoise as trickster reveal his greed, cunning, and lack of scruples. Of potential interest to children are a puzzle story, "Oliji and Her Three Suitors," and "God and the Two Brothers."

Other examples of narratives and proverbs appear in chapter 26, "Fables—Folklore—Proverbs," of the author's earlier *Among the Ibos of Nigeria,* a 1921 work reprinted by Barnes & Noble, of New York, and by Frank Cass, of London, in 1966 (DT5.5.B3 1966). Eight of the 10 untitled stories are about animals; each is didactic. Here are variants of "The Hare and the Tortoise," in which Frog races Deer, and "Tug of War," in which Tortoise pits Buffalo and Elephant against each other.

21. Canu, Gaston, *comp.*
CONTES MOSSI ACTUELS; ETUDE ETHNO-LINGUISTIQUE. Dakar, IFAN, 1969. 361 p. map. (Mémoires de l'Institut fondamental d'Afrique noire, no. 82) PL8521.C3

Text in Mossi and French.

Bibliography: p. [337]–340.

An analysis of 225 traditional tales recorded by high school

From Tales of Yoruba Gods and Heroes *by Harold Courlander, illustrated by Larry Lurin. Item 23.*

students in the capital city of Ouagadougou, Upper Volta, resulted in this compilation of 25 stories, set down both in the Mossi language and in literal French translations. They are followed by an examination of traditional tales—their genres, themes, characters, and literary and cultural values. Genres represented include the etiological, trickster, moral, and entertaining stories. "Le Prince des Paroles" and "Le Prince des Menteurs" revolve around remarkable children.

A short survey of the Mossi, their way of life and language, introduces the work.

22. Cardinall, Allan W.
 TALES TOLD IN TOGOLAND, TO WHICH IS ADDED THE MYTHICAL & TRADITIONAL HISTORY OF DAGOMBA, BY E. F. TAMAKLOE. Westport, Conn., Negro Universities Press [1970] 290 p.
 GR360.T6C3 1970

Reprint of the 1931 ed.

Myths, legends, and tales told to the author by "peasants and hunters."

In his introductory chapter the author describes the land and its inhabitants, commenting that the "real difference between African peasantry and European . . . is that the superstitions are actually believed in and not half believed in. . . . They are not mere tales to while away the evening hours; they are real happenings." He provides some one hundred stories illustrating the great range of lore: creation myths, tales of little people and Anansi, how and why narratives, cumulative stories, and didactic tales (why a woman does not choose her husband herself, why children must obey their elders). The final chapter presents the legendary history of the Dagomba people: the beginnings of totemism, stories of famine (including Tar Baby stories), and legends of rulers.

23. Courlander, Harold.
    TALES OF YORUBA GODS AND HEROES. Decorations by Larry Lurin. New York, Crown Publishers [1973] 243 p.
    GR360.Y6C68 1973

Bibliography: p. 241–243.

> EARTH AND SKY
> *Olunrete!*
> Earth and Sky
> Went hunting.
> They killed a bush rat.
> Earth claimed to be the elder,
> Sky also claimed to be the elder.
> Then Sky-owner moved away.
> The yam roots stopped growing,
> The maize gave no more kernels,
> Mothers went searching for water,
> Babies became faint and cried.
> *Lunrete!*

In a handsomely decorated work, a well-known folklorist introduces major deities of the Yoruba pantheon. Beginning with a preliminary historical sketch of the Yoruba people and their gods, the *orishas*, his stories tell of beginnings—divination and the making of land and people by Oblata, King of the White Cloth—of lesser deities, water spirits, and great heroes. Notes provide specific background for each narrative, and appendixes describe Yoruba religious traditions in the Americas, Haiti, Trinidad, and Cuba and give examples of Cuban Yoruba narratives, drum music, and songs. A glossary is also included.

24. Cronise, Florence M., *and* Henry W. Ward.
    CUNNIE RABBIT, MR. SPIDER, AND THE OTHER BEEF; WEST AFRICAN FOLK TALES. Illustrations by Gerald Sichel. Foreword by Hermese E. Roberts. Chicago, Afro-Am Press, 1969. 330 p.
    GR350.C7 1969

Reprint of the 1903 ed.

Temne animal narratives selected from 125 stories gathered from the children in a mission school. In their introduction the authors describe the method of recording the stories, as well as the traditional literature itself, and give an account of "the inner life of the African" as seen by "an educated native."

The stories center largely on animals, although a few *Märchen* are included. The authors note that human qualities and characteristics are ascribed to the various animals—Spider, Cunning Rabbit, Deer, Leopard, Turtle, Elephant, Lizard, Chameleon, Cat, and Hawk—and call attention to the importance for the native of the cunning and cleverness evidenced in narratives about these creatures. They point out the likeness of Mr. Spider to Brer Rabbit, although the former is vicious and the latter is not; to Annancy, of the West Indies; and to Hlakanyana, of South Africa. Cunning Rabbit appears more amiable and intelligent than Mr. Spider.

Rambling descriptions frame the tales, which are presented in pidgin English, their natural flow constantly interrupted by paternalistic and pedantic interpolations. The work is flawed further by an overweening sense of superiority of the white man, but it has, nevertheless, usefulness as source material for narratives for children, since all of the stories would appeal to them. Riddles are included.

25. Dayrell, Elphinstone.
FOLK STORIES FROM SOUTHERN NIGERIA, WEST AFRICA. With an introduction by Andrew Lang. New York, Negro Universities Press [1969]   xv, 158 p.   GR360.N5D18 1969

Reprint of the 1910 ed.

In his introduction to these 40 narratives gathered by a district commissioner, Andrew Lang points out likenesses to traditional lore in such cultures as the Australian and the Welsh and also identifies certain animal stories as "Just So Stories." Other tales, he notes, explain customs and illustrate morals: "Never kill a man or a woman because you are envious of their beauty, as, if you do, you will surely be punished" and "Never marry a stranger, no matter how pretty she may be." "The Woman With Two Skins," "The King's Magic Drum," and "Why the Sun and the Moon Live in the Sky" have the greatest appeal for children, the last having been retold in Blair Lent's Caldecott Medal-winning picture book of the same title.

26. Edgar, Frank.
HAUSA TALES AND TRADITIONS; an English translation of *Tatsuniyoyi na Hausa*. Translated and edited by Neil Skinner. With a foreword by M. G. Smith, v. 1. New York,

Africana Pub. Corp. [1969] xxxiv, 440 p.
GR360.H3E13, v. 1

Originally published as *Litafi na Tatsuniyoyi na Hausa*, 1911–13.
Glossary and "Table of Cross References to the Original Edition."

The first in a projected three-volume translation of Frank Edgar's *Tatsuniyoyi na Hausa*, a collection of Hausa folklore, described by M. G. Smith in his foreword as "a comprehensive body of diverse materials, much of which, being explicitly fictive, is of great ethnographic significance." Smith also discusses the work of other British officials in the field of collecting, Hausa society, and the literature itself—its genres and uses. Neil Skinner, translator, comments on the first volume of the Edgar work: "a remarkable miscellany: fables, history, quasi-history, proverbs, riddles, a few songs or poems . . . tongue-twisters." Further, he talks about the stories, their language and style, and the problems of translation.

The material is arranged in six parts: Mainly Animals—Gizo (Spider), Hare, Jackal, Lion, and Hyena; Caricatures—Ethnic and Other Stereotypes; Moralising; Men and Women, Young Men and Maidens; Dilemma Tales; and Cases At Law.

27. Ellis, Alfred B.
THE YORUBA-SPEAKING PEOPLES OF THE SLAVE COAST OF WEST AFRICA; THEIR RELIGION, MANNERS, CUSTOMS, LAWS, LANGUAGE, ETC. With an appendix containing a comparison of the Tshi, Gā, Ewe, and Yoruba languages. London, Chapman and Hall, 1894. 402 p. maps. Micro 18698 DT

A detailed study by a government official, which in part deals with the proverbs and tales of the Yorubas. In "Folk-Lore Tales" he speaks of their vast body of tales, or *alo*, and the importance of the professional storyteller, or *akpalo*, in their society. He also describes the *arokin*, or "narrator of native traditions, several of whom are attached to each king, or paramount chief, and who may be regarded as the depositaries [sic] of the ancient chronicles."

The stories include some about Tortoise "of the thousand cunning tricks," often called Ajapa the bald-headed elf, who takes the place of Anansi (Spider) as trickster. Others are *Märchen*. One of these, complete with songs, tells of a young girl who sells palm-oil to a goblin, only to find herself one cowry short. She follows him for her money.

"Oh! young palm-oil seller,
You must now turn back."
"Save I get my cowry,
I'll not leave your track."
"Oh, young palm-oil seller,
Soon will lead this track,
To the bloody river,
Then you must turn back."

This work has been reprinted by Benin Press of Chicago (DT500.E47 1964) and by Anthropological Publications of Oosterhout in The Netherlands (DT500.E47 1966).

Other studies by the author containing folklore materials include *The Ewe-Speaking Peoples of the Slave Coast of West Africa, Their Religion, Manners, Customs, Laws, Languages, etc.* (London, Chapman and Hall, 1890. 331 p. DT500.E44), reprinted by Benin Press of Chicago (DT500.E44 1965), and *The Tshi-Speaking Peoples of the Gold Coast of West Africa. Their Religion, Manners, Customs, Laws, Languages, etc.* (London, Chapman and Hall, 1887. 343 p. DT511.E48), reissued by Benin Press of Chicago (DT511.E48 1964) and by Anthropological Publications in Oosterhout, The Netherlands (DT510.42.E4 1966).

28. Ennis, Merlin, *comp. and tr.*
    UMBUNDU; FOLK TALES FROM ANGOLA. Comparative analysis by Albert B. Lord. Boston, Beacon Press [1962] 316 p.   GR360.A5E5

These narratives, taken from scripts in the Ovimbundu language by their missionary-compiler, and later translated into English, represent but a segment of "the great reservoir of yet uncollected and untranslated stories." In a preface the compiler states that he has kept the English texts as faithful as possible to the originals. In his prose selections he has not reproduced the rhythm of the Ovimbundu language; songs are rendered in their original rhythm. Dr. Albert B. Lord, professor of Yugoslav and Comparative Literature at Harvard, comments on the themes and structure of the tales and their relationships to each other.

The tales depict the complexities of relationships within the family, the community, and the animal world. A number have potential appeal for young readers because of their themes: a child at the mercy of a stepmother, a legless girl outwitting an ogre, and a young boy's rescue of his sister and her friends from cannibals.

29. Equilbecq, Victor François.
   CONTES POPULAIRES D'AFRIQUE OCCIDENTALE. Précédés d'un essai sur la littérature merveilleuse des noirs. Nouv. éd. augm. d'une ptie. inédite. Avant-propos par Robert Cornevin. Paris, G.-P. Maisonneuve et Larose, 1972. 512 p. (Les Littératures populaires de toute les nations. Nouv. sér., t. 17)   GR360.F7E65 1972

Includes bibliographical references.

An essay by Robert Cornevin, then *secrétaire perpétual de l'Académie des sciences d'outre-mer*, identifying earlier collectors and their work and including a biography of Equilbecq, introduces this rich compendium of West African narratives. The study also contains a detailed examination of folklore—its genres, relationships to other cultures, themes, characters (animal, human, and supernatural), and motifs. The tales are arranged by ethnic origin, with explanatory notes when necessary.

30. Finnegan, Ruth H., *comp.*
   LIMBA STORIES AND STORY-TELLING. Oxford, Clarendon Press, 1967. 352 p. (Oxford library of African literature)
   GR360.L6F5

Bibliography: p. [351]-352.

In the first part of this two-part work, a British scholar provides a detailed, authoritative description of the Limba people of northern Sierra Leone, their villages, rice farms, chiefs, family life, and religion. She then analyzes their oral literature, emphasizing its artistic expression, genesis, and classification, as well as the storyteller and the occasions for storytelling.

The second part consists of stories in three categories: people, Kanu ("a High God" as well as a story character) and origins (the beginnings of things), and animals. A selection of proverbs and riddles follows. Two appendixes contain texts "with word-for-word translation" and a list of narrators.

" . . . a meaty collection, providing a lavish background of the setting and the society, but flawed by inadequate comparative notes" (Richard M. Dorson, in his *African Folklore*, p. 11–12. See item 1.).

In her later *Oral Literature in Africa* (London, Clarendon Press, 1970. xix, 558 p. [Oxford library of African literature] PL8010.F5), the author provides a thorough analysis of the oral tradition.

Studies and Collections for Adults 21

From Tales for the Third Ear, from Equatorial Africa *by Verna Aardema, illustrated by Ib Ohlsson. Item 47.*

31. Gbadamosi, Bakare, *and* Ulli Beier.
NOT EVEN GOD IS RIPE ENOUGH: YORUBA STORIES. London, Heinemann Educational, 1968. 58 p. (African writers series, 48)   PZ4.G2874 No

Twenty subtly ironic narratives provide insight into West African philosophical attitudes towards human nature and its foibles. A small number with likely appeal for children include "The Pot That Boils Over Dirties Itself," retold in Olawale Idewu's *Nigerian Folk Tales* (item 35) as "The Hunter Who Was King"; "What an Old Man Can See Sitting Down—A Young Man Can't See Standing Up," a tale about the value of the aged; and "Hatred Is Like Rain in a Desert—It Is of No Use to Anybody," which deals with ingratitude.

Julius Lester has adapted two of them in his *Black Folktales* (item 188): "Large Eyes Produce Many Tears" as "The Girl With the Large Eyes" and "A Wise Man Solves His Own Problems" as "The Old Man Who Wouldn't Take Advice."

32. Graham, Lorenz B.
 How God fix Jonah. Wood engravings by Letterio Calapai. New York, Reynal & Hitchcock [1946] xvi, 171 p.
 GR350.G7

A selection of Bible stories told "in the speech patterns and images of African people." The author discusses both the idiom of the West African, which he heard in Liberia, and the stories, which have been "set down as an African lad might tell them to his friends." Commenting on pronunciation and rhythm, he defines such words as "palaver" and "pican." A volume produced with many striking wood engravings.

Five of the stories have appeared as individual picture books, all published in New York by Crowell: *Every Man Heart Lay Down*, with pictures by Colleen Browning (1970), the story of the Nativity; *A Road Down in the Sea*, with pictures by Gregorio Prestopino (1970), the story of the Exodus; *David He No Fear*, with pictures by Ann Grifalconi (1971), the story of David and Goliath; *God Wash the World and Start Again*, with pictures by Clare Romano Ross (1971), the story of Noah and the flood; and *Hongry Catch the Foolish Boy*, with pictures by James Brown, Jr. (1973), the parable of the prodigal son.

33. Herskovits, Melville J., *and* Frances S. Herskovits.
 Dahomean narrative; a cross-cultural analysis. Evanston [Ill.] Northwestern University Press [1958] xvi, 490 p. (Northwestern University, Evanston, Ill. African studies, no. 1) GR360.D3H4

"To extend the knowledge of African literary resources and to dispel the notions that Africans tell only simple animal stories," two well-known anthropologists have selected 132 *hwendo* (myths) and *heho* (tales) for their study of the Dahomean oral tradition. These are preceded by a description of the authors' methodology, an examination of narrative forms, classification scheme (including riddles, proverbs, and verse), themes, values, and style, and a discussion of a "cross-cultural approach to myth."

Narratives follow grouped as: exploits of the gods; divination; hunter stories; *enfant terrible* tales—about twins, orphans, and the abnormally born; Yo stories—about a conniving, gluttonous, impulsive being spiritually akin to Spider and Hare; historical tales; tales of women—about love, intrigue, and betrayal; explanatory and moralizing tales; and miscellaneous tales. Each area opens with a list of *dramatis personae*. Explanatory footnotes are employed when necessary. Hunter stories and *enfant terrible* tales are valuable sources for a reteller.

34. Herzog, George, *and* Charles G. Blooah.
JABO PROVERBS FROM LIBERIA; MAXIMS IN THE LIFE OF A NATIVE TRIBE. London, Oxford University Press, 1936. 272 p.   PN6519.J15H4

The numbered proverbs and sayings which compose this work are grouped as Proverbs: 1) Nature (Phenomena of Nature, Plants, Invertebrates, Fish, Amphibians and Reptiles, Birds, Mammals); 2) Culture (Food and Tobacco, Objects of Use, Human Behavior and Pursuits, Social Relations); 3) People (Types, Attributes, The Human Body); and Sayings: Sayings Similar to Proverbs, Definitions, Descriptive Sayings, and Idiomatic Sayings.

Recorded by the author and his Liberian assistant while conducting a study of music and signaling for the Department of Anthropology of the University of Chicago, the texts appear here first in the original language, with an interlinear translation, and then in English. Each is defined. Parables or stories explain the proverb or saying in some instances. One of these, "One does not see the coming of sleep," appears in expanded form as "The One You Don't See Coming" in Courlander's *The Cow-Tail Switch* (item 51). Other examples of Herzog's parables with storytelling possibilities are saying 81, ". . . one doesn't shake hands with a crowd," which is included in *The Cow-Tail Switch* as "Don't Shake Hands With Everybody"; and saying 95, in which "Tortoise says: one person alone has no wisdom." The latter, often found as a story with Ananse or Tortoise as hero, explains why knowledge and wisdom are scattered throughout the world.

An introduction discusses the role of the proverb and its related forms in African society. Appendixes list proverbs and sayings accompanied by parables or stories, sources, and a comparison of Jabo (Grebo) and Kru proverbs. A subject index is provided.

From Tales of Mogho; African Stories from Upper Volta *by Frederic Guirma. Item 58.*

35. Idewu, Olawale, *and* Omotayo Adu.
NIGERIAN FOLK TALES. Told to and edited by Barbara K. and Warren S. Walker. Text decorations by Margaret Barbour. New Brunswick, N.J., Rutgers University Press [1961] 113 p. GR360.N5I3

Thirty-seven Yoruba tales "taken almost entirely verbatim from oral renditions" were told to the editors by two young college students from Nigeria. In their richly informative introduction the editors describe the backgrounds of the students, Mr. Idewu, a Christian convert, and Mr. Adu, a Muslim. They throw light upon the Nigerian dramatic tradition in storytelling and "the alteration of traditional tales to fit the demands of a changing cultural situation," e.g., use of a bed instead of a sleeping mat, wives sharing one house with their husband instead of each having her own, and husbands and wives eating together, formerly forbidden. They comment further that the tales retold by the Christian show greater changes than those retold by the Muslim.

The editors have followed the Thompson index of types "as much as possible" in their groupings of the narratives into Tales of Demon Lovers; Pourquoi Stories; Moral Fables; Trickster Tales; and Fertility Tales. They point out characteristics of each category, explaining their commentary in the notes (p. 77–109), and include a bibliography (111–113).

Small linoleum block prints, based on photographs of Nigerian art objects, add to the interest and attractiveness of the book.

36. Itayemi, Phebean, *and* Percival Gurrey, *comps.*
    FOLK TALES AND FABLES. London, Penguin Books [1953]
    122 p. (Penguin West African series, WA3) GR350.I8

In their preface to this collection of West African narratives, the compilers note that the Yoruba tales "have been more carefully selected and translated . . . [whereas] most of the others have been got together as time and occasion allowed, and they have been kept unchanged, as the translators remembered them, without being 'written up' to make them more interesting or more attractive. It should be borne in mind that the translators of many of these stories . . . are unskilled in translating and are not professional storytellers."

Continuing their examination of folk tales in the introduction, the compilers contend that the translations have lost "two important things . . . many of the jokes and the puns, and the funny twists of language that the listeners originally enjoyed . . . [along with] the special songs that are so often part of them, especially those of the Yorubas." Thus "these Englished folk stories from West Africa are without their distinctive African dress" and are "merely the *plain*" stories. Further, they discuss the background of the tales and reflection of the traditions and ideals of the peoples. Three recurrent themes—the value of knowledge, the importance of good social behavior, and the upbringing of children—are discussed.

The collection is arranged by people and area: Yoruba Stories, Isoko Stories, Gold Coast Stories, and Sierra Leone Stories. The Yoruba are classified by genre.

A useful source for research.

37. Johnston, Hugh A. S., *ed. and tr.*
    A SELECTION OF HAUSA STORIES. Oxford, Clarendon Press, 1966. 241 p. (Oxford library of African literature)
    PL8234.Z95E5 1966

Appendix in Hausa.

A former British official in Nigeria, Johnston has drawn more than half of the 86 narratives in this text from Frank Edgar's *Tatsuniyoyi na Hausa,* a three-volume work in Hausa—"easily the largest repository of folktales to be found in any African language."

In his introduction he surveys Hausa society and examines the Hausa language and the work of collectors, in particular John Alder Burton and Frank Edgar. He comments on the antiquity of the tales, their significance, general characteristics of each genre, and dramatic presentation.

The tales are arranged as follows: The Animal Stories, The Fairy Tales, Historical Legends and Fragments, True Stories, and Fiction. Proverbs and Aphorisms also form a section. The appendix consists of six tales in the Hausa language. Each narrative has an appended note that provides source information and, when necessary, citation of textual alterations and explanatory material. Parallels to Brer Rabbit stories are specified.

Three tricksters share the role of protagonist in the animal stories: the cunning, malevolent, and ruthless Spider, of the Sudanic peoples; the sly, resourceful, and generally sagacious Jackal, of the Hamites; and the mischievously clever Hare, of the "Bantu" (encountered less frequently than the other two). The author notes that Zomo (Hare) is so unquestionably one of Brer Rabbit's grandfathers that he has taken a small liberty with the translation and called him Rabbit.

The fairytales abound in djinns, ogres, mysterious old women, and shape-changers (animal and human). A number of these, like "The Girl and the Frog and the Chief's Son," a Cinderella variant, resemble well-known European favorites.

Flavor is added throughout by the retention of such phrases as "God grant you forgiveness," the standard greeting for a man of learning.

38. Nassau, Robert H.
WHERE ANIMALS TALK: WEST AFRICAN FOLK LORE TALES.
New York, Negro Universities Press [1970, c1912] 250 p.
GR350.N3 1970

The author notes in his preface that the typical native African *Ekano,* or legend, is marked by repetition and is "of very ancient origin . . . in supposed prehistoric times, when Beasts and Human Beings are asserted to have lived together with social relations in the same community. . . . The most distinctive feature of these Tales is that, while the actors are Beasts, they are speaking and living as Human Beings, acting as a beast in a human environment; and, instantly, in the same sentence, acting as a human being in a beast's environment." He comments also on the prevalence of a "powerful personal fetish-charm known as 'Ngalo'; a fetish almost as valuable as Aladdin's Lamp of the Arabian Nights," points out possible Arabic influences, and describes the setting for storytelling: "At night, all gather around the camp-fire; and the Tales are told with, at intervals, accompaniment of drum; and parts of the plot are illustrated by an appropriate song, or by a short dance, the platform being only the earth, and the scenery the forest shadows and the moon or stars."

The collection, predominantly animal tales, is divided into three parts representing the Mpongwe, Benga, and Fang peoples. Each section has a short introduction, and each tale is preceded by the *dramatis personae* and an explanatory note. An index supplies a list of the animal names then used in West Africa.

39. Niane, Djibril T.
    SUNDIATA: AN EPIC OF OLD MALI. Translated by G. D. Pickett. [London] Longmans [1965] 96 p. map. (Forum series)   DT532.2.N513

Translation of Soundjata.

> I am a griot. It is I, Djeli Mamoudou Kouyaté, son of Bintou Kouyaté and Djeli Kedian Kouyaté, master in the art of eloquence. Since time immemorial the Kouyatés have been in the service of the Keita princes of Mali; we are vessels of speech, we are the repositories which harbour secrets many centuries old. . . . without us the names of kings would vanish into oblivion, we are the memory of mankind; by the spoken word we bring to life the deeds and exploits of kings for younger generations. . . . Listen then, sons of Mali, children of the black people, listen to my word, for I am going to tell you of Sundiata, the father of the Bright Country, of the savanna land, the ancestor of those who draw the bow, the master of a hundred vanquished kings.

Thus begins the epic of Sundiata, which recounts his birth, childhood misfortunes, and rise to greatness as a warrior and the founder of the empire of Mali. The author heard this hero tale first from "an obscure griot" (a bard-storyteller) and subsequently translated it into French. Comparable to epics of India and the western world, this story has interest for children. For a variant adapted to young people, see Bertol's *Sundiata: The Epic of the Lion King* (item 50).

40. Rattray, Robert S.
AKAN-ASHANTI FOLK-TALES. Illustrated by Africans of the Gold Coast Colony. Oxford, Clarendon Press, 1930. xx, 275 p. plates. GR360.A55R3

Seventy-five Ghanaian tales, "the gleanings, if not of 'a thousand and one nights,' at least of many scores of evenings spent sitting in a circle after dark in the village street or, if in the rains, in some open *pato* (three-walled room) with the four sides of the *gyase kesie* (big courtyard) of the compound thronged with villagers gathered under the dripping eaves to hear and to relate these tales." The narratives, rendered in the vernacular and accompanied by Twi texts, have a preface in which the author describes his method of collecting and translating them. Further, he explains their origin, nature, role in society, and classification.

In these vigorous and entertaining stories—whether droll, cumulative, moral, or how and why—the world of men and animals come together. Anansi, sometimes man, sometimes spider, is the hero (or antihero) of most of the tales. The tellings are pleasing in their rhythmic presentation. Formula beginnings and endings, Twi words and colloquialisms such as "old-woman-grandmother," interpolated songs and refrains, and ideophones—words like "f're! f're! f're!" to express the swishing sound of a leopard's tail—create a sense of atmosphere.

One of the sources used by Harold Courlander, the collection offers much to any reteller. Here, as an example, is the beginning of "How It Came About That Children Were (First) Whipped":

> They say that (once upon a time) a great famine came, and that Father Ananse, the Spider, and his wife Aso, and his children, Ntikuma, Nyiwankonfwea (Thin-shanks), Afudotwedotwe (Belly-like-to-burst), and Tikonokono (Big-big-head), built a little settlement and lived in it. Every day the Spider used to go and bring food, wild yams, and they boiled and ate them. Now one day, Father Ananse went to the bush; he saw that a beautiful dish was standing there. He said, "This dish is beautiful." The dish said, "My name is not beautiful." The Spider said, "What are you called?" It replied, "I am called 'Fill-up-some-and-eat.'"

Black-and-white drawings and halftone plates by a team of 12 young African artists harmonize with the text.

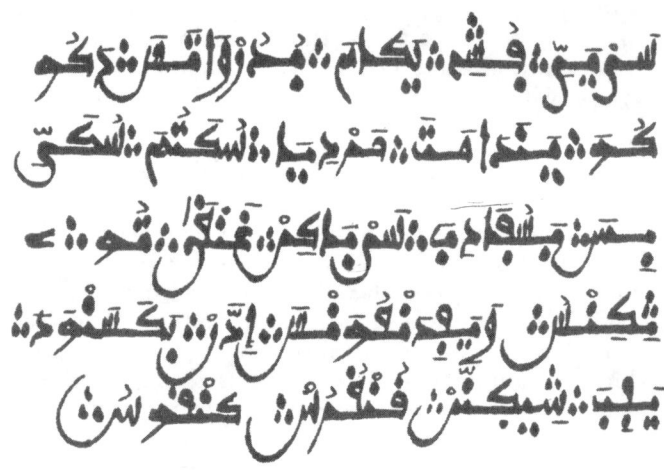

Hausa writing, from Hausa Folk-Lore, Customs, Proverbs, Etc., *by Robert Sutherland Rattray. Item 41.*

41. ——, ed. and tr.
   HAUSA FOLK-LORE, CUSTOMS, PROVERBS, ETC. Collected and transliterated with English translation and notes. With a preface by R. R. Marett. New York, Negro Universities Press [1969] 2 v. illus.   PL8234.A2R3 1969

Transliterated text with English translation and Hausa text on opposite pages.

Reprint of the 1913 ed.

Contents: v. 1. Preface. Author's note. Alphabet. pt. 1. A short history, purporting to give the origin of the Hausa nation and the story of their conversion to the Mohammedan religion. pt. 2. Stories in which people are the heroes and heroines. Illustrations.—v. 2. pt. 3. Animal stories. pt. 4. Customs and art. pt. 5. Proverbs. pt. 6. Notes. Illustrations.

A study of the Hausa language by an assistant district commissioner in the former Gold Coast, also an anthropologist-folklorist-linguist.

The volume is prefaced by comment from R. R. Marett, then a reader in social anthropology at Exeter. He describes the author's method of recording the tales as having had them dictated to him by a *mālam* (scribe) "of the best class," who knew Arabic and possessed literary skill.

Rattray points out that many of the tales "involved, first, a translation from Arabic into Hausa; secondly, a transliteration of the Hausa writing; and thirdly, a translation into English from the Hausa." Thus original form and flavor have been preserved.

Much of the material here is not suitable for children but is valuable for the student of African folklore. The narratives, as presented, clearly convey the original style of telling. Formula beginnings and endings enhance the atmosphere of the stories:

> A story, a story. This tale is about a maiden. A certain man had three children, two boys and a girl. . . . This is a story about orphans. A story, a story. Let it go, let it come. A certain man . . . That is all. Off with the rat's head. And the moral of all this is, if you see a man is poor do not despise him; you do not know but that some day he may be better than you. That is all. Off with the rat's head.

The tale content varies. A number of stories center about orphans, mysteries like a baby pumpkin with an insatiable appetite that swallows all in its way, a magic spoon called "Help me," a talking thigh-bone, and animals. Spider tales predominate. Muslim influences are evident in such expressions as "They adjured her by Allah and the Prophet . . ." and "for the sake of Allah and the prophets look after her well for me."

42. Schön, James F., *ed. and tr.*
MAGÁNA HAUSA. NATIVE LITERATURE, OR PROVERBS, TALES, FABLES, AND HISTORICAL FRAGMENTS IN THE HAUSA LANGUAGE. To which is added a translation in English. London, Society for Promoting Christian Knowledge, 1885-86. 2 v. in 1. PL8234.S35

Vol. 2 has special title page: *African Proverbs, Tales and Historical Fragments.*
Contents: [v.1] Introductory sentences. Proverbs. Letters of Dorŭgu. The life and travels of Dòrŭgu, accompanying the late Dr. H. Barth in Africa, England, and Germany, as dictated by himself. Narratives, tales, and descriptions, chiefly by Dorŭgu. Contributions forwarded to the author by the Reverend J. C. John, native minister at Lokojah, river Niger. Contributions forwarded to the author by Mr. G. A. Krause, from Tripoli, in Africa.—[v. 2] English translation.

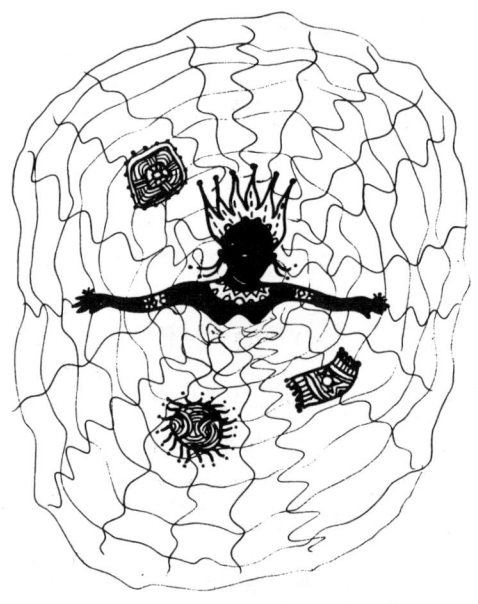

From Abayomi Fuja's Fourteen Hundred Cowries, and Other African Tales, *illustrated by Ademola Olugebefola. Item 56.*

A body of lore set down by a missionary in the last quarter of the 19th century to give students of the Hausa language a connected literature in their own tongue and enable them to become familiar with it through the medium of their own language. The texts reveal much about Hausa beliefs and attitudes, for example, about women and slavery, and also show Muslim influences. The genres include *Märchen,* animal tales, stories depicting family and public life, and drolls, one of which, "The Story of a Mother and Her Obedient Son," is a variant of "Prudent Hans" and "Epaminondas."

43. Talbot, Percy A.
 IN THE SHADOW OF THE BUSH. London, W. Heinemann, 1912. [New York, Negro Universities Press, 1969] xiv, 500 p. illus., fold. map. GN653.T3 1969

A work undertaken "first, for the pleasure of it, and secondly, because primitive races, the world over, are changing so rapidly that it seemed well to place on record the story of a people most of whom were untouched by white influence . . . in 1907. . . . It has been written in the intervals of official work, during marches which averaged 1700 miles a year, when an uninterrupted half-hour was a thing, longed for, but unattainable." Following a brief foreword, the author examines lifestyles, religious beliefs, and customs of the Ekoi of Nigeria.

In chapter 31 Talbot turns his attention to the folklore itself. Most of his tales are animal and how and why; or etiological, stories, such as "Why a Murderer Should Die in the Same Way as His Victim," a variant of the English "Binnorie" and the German "Singing Bone." Commenting on resemblances to the *Arabian Nights* stories "The Treasure House in the Bush" and "Ali Baba and the Forty Thieves," he points out such stock characters as "the Woman covered with Sores who meets all travellers to the nether world, and helps to success, or dooms to failure, according to whether their goodness of heart is such to pass her tests"; the Lame Boy "who plays the part of 'Good Fairy' wherever he appears, enacting a Prometheus-like role in 'How Fire First Came on Earth' "; and Sheep and Tortoise who are "credited with cunning above all other animals, and hold in this respect somewhat the position of Brer Rabbit."

44. Tremearne, Arthur J. N.
HAUSA SUPERSTITIONS AND CUSTOMS; AN INTRODUCTION TO THE FOLK-LORE AND THE FOLK. With a new introductory note by Mervyn Hiskett. [London] F. Cass, 1970. xxi, 548 p. illus., fold. map. (Cass library of African studies. General studies, no. 90)   GN653.T7 1970

A three-part study, first published in 1913. In part one the author, a former government official, examines folklore, its importance, nature, characters (a chapter is devoted to animals and their world), and style. He comments also on problems of collecting, narrators, and such printed sources in Hausa as Frank Edgar's *Litafi na Tatsuniyoyi na Hausa*, a work being translated into English by Neil Skinner (item 26). At considerable length he analyzes the supernatural world of gods, spirits, monsters, fantastic beasts, and witches. Riddles, proverbs, and poetry receive some attention.

The animal tales are obviously related to those in Uncle Remus and those in *Cunnie Rabbit, Mr. Spider, and the Other Beef,* a collection of Sierra Leone stories (item 24). The kinship of other tales to familiar European, Indian, and Arabian narratives is equally apparent. There is a Cinderella tale in "The Tender-Hearted Maiden and the Fish"; a Tar

Baby in "The Deceitful Spider, the Half-Man, and the Rubber Girl"; and a Jack the Giant Killer in "How Aula Killed Dodo." Most of the trickster tales have Gizo (Spider) as hero, although Zomo (Hare) appears in a few.

The second part comprises 100 narratives, accompanied by footnotes citing sources, parallels, and variants. These represent *Märchen*, animal stories, and stories of everyday life. Part three offers additional background about customs and beliefs.

The whole is a rich and useful resource for the storyteller. In "The Slave Who Was Wiser Than the King," for example, we read:

> Immediately You-are-wiser-than-the-King galloped back and saluted the King, and said, "Who is the equal of You-are-wiser-than-the-King?" Then the King answered, "I am," and he jumped up to seize him, but You-are-wiser-than-the-King changed himself into a Frog. Then the King changed himself into a Snake to swallow the Frog, but You-are-wiser-than-the-King became a Mouse. Then the King changed himself into a Cat, but the other become a Red-bird, and the King became a Hawk. The Red-Bird flew against an Old Woman who was sweeping the courtyard, and fell into her eye, and became the pupil, then the King became the eyebrow. And even now they are like that, the pupil of the eye is afraid to come out lest the eyebrow should catch him. That is the end.

45. ———.
THE TAILED HEAD-HUNTERS OF NIGERIA; AN ACCOUNT OF AN OFFICIAL'S SEVEN YEARS' EXPERIENCE IN THE NORTHERN NIGERIAN PAGAN BELT, AND A DESCRIPTION OF THE MANNERS, HABITS, AND CUSTOMS OF THE NATIVE TRIBES. With 38 illustrations & a map. London, Seeley Service, 1912. XVI, 341 p. plates. DT515.T8

The final chapter of this report presents seven Hausa narratives: "The Mallan, the Spider, and the Hyena"; "The Spider, the Fish, and the Lion"; "The Hyena, the Sheep, and the Monkey"; "The Donkey-Girl"; "Dodo, the Spider, and His Wives"; "Salifu and the Wonderful Mare"; and "The Greedy Woman and the Good Bird." General comments on Hausa folklore, the animal tales in particular, precede the texts. "The Donkey-Girl" is a Swan Maiden tale. In "Salifu and the Wonderful Mare" the horse plays the familiar role of the fairy godmother.

For the author's comprehensive study of folklore, see his *Hausa Superstitions and Customs* (item 44).

From Tales for the Third Ear, from Equatorial Africa *by Verna Aardema, illustrated by Ib Ohlsson. Item 47.*

COLLECTIONS FOR CHILDREN

46. Aardema, Verna.
 TALES FROM THE STORY HAT. Illustrated by Elton Fax. New York, Coward-McCann [1960] 72 p. PZ8.1.A213 Tal

In an introduction, Augusta Baker, then storytelling and group work specialist at the New York Public Library, comments on the impact of modern civilization on Africa, on the greater importance once given to storytelling, and on the narratives themselves. A product of the author's "life-long" interest in Africa, the book contains explanatory stories, trickster tales featuring Hare and Anansi, and tales of men, clever and stupid, good and bad. All merit a place in the story

WEST AFRICA

From Sundiata: The Epic of the Lion King *by* Roland Bertol, *illustrated by* Gregorio Prestopino. *Item 50.*

hour today. Elton Fax's soft-pencil drawings evoke the mood of the narratives.

Notes on the stories, a bibliography, and a glossary are appended.

Eleven more West African tales of wit and wisdom appear in a sequel, *More Tales From the Story Hat,* illustrated by Elton Fax (New York, Coward-McCann [c1966] 72 p. PZ8.1.A213).

47. ———.
TALES FOR THE THIRD EAR, FROM EQUATORIAL AFRICA. Drawings by Ib Ohlsson. New York, Dutton [1969] 96 p. illus. (part col.)   PZ8.1.A213 Taj

In a short foreword the reteller suggests the stories' setting by describing the start of an evening storytelling session:

> "Kunnenka nawa?" (How many ears have you?) The people answer, "Kunnena biyu!" (We have two ears!) The narrator says, "Kara na uku, ka sha labari!" (Add a third, and listen to what I have to tell you!)

She adds that she has retold the tales from those recorded word-for-word from Hausa, Masai, and Swahili storytellers and cites a source for each one.

The author has kept to basic story outlines although she has provided explanatory details and has omitted unattractive incidents. Her style is informal, incorporating colloquial dialog and African names for such characters as Gitojo the Hare and Nelotu the Lioness. The animals themselves and the description of setting convey a sense of place.

She has freely adapted three stories as picture books, all published in New York by Coward-McCann in 1960. *The Sky-God Stories* ([32] p. PZ8.1.A213 Sk) tells how Ananse won the Ashanti stories for his own. Another Ashanti tale, *The Na of Wa* ([32] p. PZ8.1.A213 Na), is about a youth who won a chieftainship with the aid of a magic ring and the animals he befriended. A Nuer tale, *Otwe* ([32] p. PZ8.1.A213 Ot), reveals the predicament of a man who is given a magic feather enabling him to understand the thoughts of animals. Elton Fax's soft-pencil, humorous illustrations capture the flavor in each.

48. Appiah, Peggy.
    ANANSE THE SPIDER: TALES FROM AN ASHANTI VILLAGE.
    Pictures by Peggy Wilson. [New York] Pantheon Books
    [1966] 152 p.   PZ8.1.A647 An

Contents: 1. How Kwaku Ananse won a kingdom with a grain of corn.—2. Kwaku Ananse and the greedy lion.—3. How the pig got his snout.—4. Why the lizard stretches his neck.—5. Kwaku Ananse and the whipping cord.—6. Kwaku Ananse and the donkey.—7. How the lion rewarded the mouse's kindness.—8. How Kwaku Ananse became bald.—9. How Kwaku Ananse destroyed a kingdom.—10. Kwaku Ananse and the rain maker.—11. Why the spider has a narrow waist.—12. Why Kwaku Ananse stays on the ceiling.—13. How wisdom was spread throughout the world.

The stories, retold by a teacher, have been rendered into colloquial language. Filling in skeletal outlines, she has provided the young reader with background material and has done so unobtrusively. She has omitted traditional beginnings and endings and distasteful or problem elements. Although no sources have been cited, it can be seen that variants of a few of the tales appear in Rattray's *Akan-Ashanti Folk-Tales* (item 40). For example, "How Kwaku Ananse Won a Kingdom With a Grain of Corn" is found in Rattray as "How

Ananse, the Spider, Became Poor," and "How Wisdom Was Spread Throughout the World" as his "How It Came About That Wisdom Came Among the Tribe."

Peggy Wilson's use of African motifs in pictures and borders makes an attractive volume.

The author has produced three other volumes of Ashanti tales: *Tales of an Ashanti Father* ([London] Deutsch [1967] 157 p. PZ8.1.A647 Tal), *The Pineapple Child, and Other Tales From Ashanti* ([London] Deutsch [1969] 173 p. PZ8.1.A647 Pi), and *The Children of Ananse* (London, Evans [1968] 176 p. PZ7.A646 Ch), all illustrated in effective scratchboard technique by Mora Dickson. Six of the stories in *The Pineapple Child* appeared first in *Ananse the Spider*, as did four of those in *Tales of an Ashanti Father*. *The Children of Ananse*, a fantasy about Ananse's descendants, also contains some of the stories.

49. Arkhurst, Joyce C.
   THE ADVENTURES OF SPIDER; WEST AFRICAN FOLK TALES.
   Illustrated by Jerry Pinkney. Boston, Little, Brown [1964]
   58 p.   PZ9.1.A7 Ad

A brief introduction describing the village scene at night, the storyteller, and Spider, "a favorite person in the stories of West Africa . . . because he is just like a naughty little boy," sets the stage for these six stories. Spider is presented without his maliciousness and lack of scruples.

Chosen for the young child, the tales include "How Spider Got a Thin Waist," "Why Spider Lives in Ceilings," "How Spider Got a Bald Head," "How Spider Helped a Fisherman," "Why Spiders Live in Dark Corners" (a variant of the Tar Baby tale), and "How the World Got Wisdom." The telling is informal and conversational, more American than African. "Why Spiders Live in Ceilings" includes a talking house episode reminiscent of "The Jackal and the Crocodile":

> "Ho! my banana-leaf house!"
> Nobody answered. . . .
> "That's funny," said Spider loudly, "my little house always answers me when I call her. I wonder what is wrong."

The lavish illustrations, some in color, are modern interpretations that lack African feeling.

50. Bertol, Roland.
SUNDIATA: THE EPIC OF THE LION KING, retold. Illustrated by Gregorio Prestopino. New York, Crowell [1970] 81 p.
PZ8.1.B4194 Su

For his retelling, the author notes: "I have relied upon several thirteenth-century Arab texts; upon unpublished manuscripts, plays, and fragments which my Malian friends gave me; and to a lesser extent upon published fragments" and a recent edition edited by D. T. Niane (item 39) of the epic as told in the town of Djeliba Koro.

The epic divides naturally into 11 short books chronicling the beginnings of Mali; the rise in Sosso of Sumanguru, the "warrior king" who made a pact with the "unholy demons of the earth and sky"; the enmity between the people of Mali and Sosso; the birth of Mari Diata, ugly, lame 12th son of the King of Mali, and his rise from the dust on which he crawled to become the destroyer of Sumanguru and the builder of the great empire of ancient Mali. Filled with more magical elements than those in the Niani version, picturing drama, courage, and chivalry, and distinguished by a clear bardic style, this work, the first of its kind from Africa for children, is a valuable addition to collections of heroic literature.

51. Courlander, Harold, *and* George Herzog.
THE COW-TAIL SWITCH, AND OTHER WEST AFRICAN STORIES. Drawings by Madye Lee Chastain. New York, Holt [1947] 143 p.   PZ8.1.C8 Co

Twenty-seven stories taken primarily from the Ashanti, Mende, and Soninke peoples of West Africa. The narratives are varied, representing the how and why stories, parables, trickster or Anansi tales, and dilemma and ironic stories, such as "Kassa, the Strong One":

> Once among the Mende people in the country known as the Sudan there was a strong man named Kassa Kena Genanina.
> "I am a strong man," he said, "the strongest man alive, and I'm not afraid of anything."

"Africa Is Many Things" and notes on the stories provide explanatory details, sources, and variants.

52. Courlander, Harold, *and* Albert Kofi Prempeh.
THE HAT-SHAKING DANCE, AND OTHER TALES FROM THE GOLD

COAST. Illustrated by Enrico Arno. New York, Harcourt,
Brace [1957] 115 p. PZ8.1.C8 Hat

From the Ashanti people of Ghana come these 21 "Anansesem" stories, half of them with Anansi the Spider as hero or antihero. Compiled by a folklorist with the assistance of a West African, the collection has an introduction describing the Ashanti civilization, as well as concluding notes on the stories. Here, Mr. Courlander describes Anansi's role as trickster hero, his place in Ashanti society, and the human and animal worlds in which the stories take place. He also names Anansi's West Indian and South American counterparts: "Aunt Nancy," "Sister Nancy," "Bouki," and "Ti-Malice." Finally, he comments on each story, supplying background information, variants, and such published sources as Capt. Robert S. Rattray's *Akan-Ashanti Folk-Tales* (item 40) and Allan W. Cardinall's *Tales Told in Togoland* (item 22).

53. Courlander, Harold, *and* Ezekiel A. Eshugbayi, *comps.*
OLODE THE HUNTER, AND OTHER TALES FROM NIGERIA. Illustrated by Enrico Arno. New York, Harcourt, Brace & World [1968] 153 p. PZ8.1.C8 Ol

A Western Nigerian collection of Yoruba tales, also containing several from the Ibo and Hausa. A number present Ijapa the Tortoise, a Yoruba trickster akin to Anansi the Spider and Brer Terrapin. Other types include the legend, or *itan,* the creation myth, and the how and why story.

In a final section of notes on the stories, the folklorist-author discusses the dual role of Ijapa in Yoruba society as "a kind of yardstick against which human behavior, human foibles, and moral strength are measured" and also as "a projection of evil forces against which mankind must contend, sometimes winning, sometimes losing." Thus Ijapa appears not only in tales but also in sayings, songs, and such proverbs as "Though Ijapa has no legs on the ground, he has wisdom in his head. (A person who is deficient in one quality may be strong in another.)" Yoruba legends and creation myths are also discussed.

Additional material on sources and counterparts is found in notes for the individual stories.

54. Creel, J. Luke, *and* Bai Gai Kiahon.
FOLK TALES OF LIBERIA. Illustrated by Carol Hoorn

Fraser. Minneapolis, T. S. Denison [1960] 144 p.
GR360.L5C7

The author states that in his translation he has not deviated from the original of these stories in plot, thought, and purpose and that he has used conventional and colloquial English to retain the mood and flavor of the original tales. The Honorable Oscar S. Norman, in 1960 when he was Assistant Secretary of the Interior of Liberia, in charge of the Department of Folkways, said that ". . . the authors have preserved the spirit and the thought purpose in the original as nearly as is possible to literature transferred to another language."

The rhythmic narratives deal with such themes as childlessness, unselfishness, beauty, friendship, arrogance, and greed. Each has a moral, sometimes stated at the opening of a story as in "The Handsome Young Man": "Too much beauty has often become an inconvenience to the man or woman who possesses it. And this is what this story is about." "The Great Race" is a variant of "The Hare and the Tortoise," except that here a deer suffers the consequences of pride. The well-known tricksters—Tortoise, Spider, and Cunning Rabbit—enter a number of the tales.

Incorporated songs and soft charcoal drawings give variety to the pages and add to the general attractiveness of the volume.

55. Dorliae, Peter G.
ANIMALS MOURN FOR DA LEOPARD, AND OTHER WEST AFRICAN TALES. Illustrated by S. Irein Wangboje. Indianapolis, Bobbs-Merrill [1970] 68 p.   PZ8.1.D746 An

The 10 stories and proverbs in this slim volume were selected and translated by a paramount chief of the Yarwin-Mehnsonoh Chiefdom, Lower Nimba County, Liberia. The narratives, all but two about animals, are occasionally earthy and didactic in tone: "Fo-Fo learned that we must reap what we sow. Fo-Fo now hangs, while ants struggle to reach him." A few are about two well-known tricksters, Spider and Turtle. "The Monkey and the Snail" is a variant of "The Hare and the Tortoise." "We Oppose President Stomach"—a tale of the rebellion of the parts of the body against the rule of President Stomach—represents a type of story less familiar to western culture.

Appended are "Some Proverbs":

> If a dog is praised for hunting, he is likely to hunt for leopard. (Too much praising makes some people try to

do things beyond their abilities.)

Spirited woodcuts by a Nigerian artist evoke the African scene and village life.

56. Fuja, Abayomi, *comp.*
    FOURTEEN HUNDRED COWRIES, AND OTHER AFRICAN TALES. With an introduction by Anne Pellowski. Illustrated by Ademola Olugebefola. New York, Lothrop, Lee & Shepard Co. [1971] 256 p.   GR360.Y6F8 1971

Animal tales and *Märchen* make up the Yoruba stories in this fresh Nigerian collection. Many originate in the "Country of the Animals," where beasts enact the roles of men and, on occasion, have encounters with humans; some are etiological; others point a moral: "If you have a friend do not try to fight him even if you think you know his secrets." Beginnings such as "There was a time when no rain fell upon the earth and the crops did not grow . . ." and "Once, many years ago, there was a great famine in the Country of the Animals . . ." reflect the ever constant threat of drought and starvation. The narratives are seasoned with songs like this:

> Oluweri, Oluweri, Goddess of the River,
> I have now returned with eyes of silver and hair
>   like stars
> Oh, if it be that my husband is dead,
> Let the face of the river run blood red,
> Or if my husband yet lives, let him come to the
>   surface,
> There he will behold his loved one they sent
>   cruelly away.

Mr. Olugebefola's ink drawings in strong line enhance the African character and attractiveness of the volume.

57. Guillot, René.
    AFRICAN FOLK TALES. Selected and translated by Gwen Marsh. Illustrated by William Papas. New York, F. Watts [1965, c1964] 160 p.   GR350.G8 1965

A selection of 23 stories freely translated from Guillot's *La Biche noire, La Brousse et la bête, Aux pays des bêtes,* and *Nouveaux contes d'Afrique,* all of which had been produced by the author, a French schoolteacher, during the 20 years he lived in West Africa. They convey little if any of the original

From Princess of the Full Moon *by Frederic Guirma. See item 58.*

African style. Only names and species of animals and birds suggest their background. However, a number of plots are unusual. "The 'Do-Good' Genie," about a leper who encountered a genie in the form of the firebird and was cured on condition that he guard the bird's eggs, ends less conclusively than most African taboo tales, since the violation of trust here is not followed by the leper's restoration to his former condition. No sources are cited.

William Papas' effective ink drawings are full of action.

58. Guirma, Frederic.
TALES OF MOGHO; AFRICAN STORIES FROM UPPER VOLTA. New York, Macmillan [1971] 113 p. illus. GR360.M65G8

Eight tales from the Mossi people are presented to young readers much as the author, today a member of the Upper

From Tales of Mogho. *Item 58.*

Volta delegation to the United Nations, heard them as a boy. A foreword by Prof. Elliott P. Skinner, of Columbia University, notes that these stories are "published here for the first time in any language."

The collection consists of one *kibare*, or myth, and seven *soalema*, or fairytales, only two of the latter being animal stories. The *kibare* tells of Naba Zid-Wende, the "They" who reign over the Kingdom of Everlasting Truth and created the earth and all that dwell therein. In its account of the efforts of Wéogho, a magician, and his friend, Tanga, to rescue their families from slavery, "Magic and Friendship" contains certain elements common to the European "Master and His Pupil." The stories are fresh and reflect the customs and traditions of the Mossi peoples and their attitude towards age and authority. African names and words have been retained. A glossary translates 64 words and expressions from the Moré (Mossi) language. The author's black-and-white drawings complement the text.

Guirma has also published in picture-book form the folk tale *Princess of the Full Moon* ([New York] Macmillan [1969, c1970] PZ8.1.G949 Pr), translated from the French by John Garrett.

59. Jablow, Alta.
GASSIRE'S LUTE; A WEST AFRICAN EPIC. Translated and adapted by Alta Jablow. Illustrated by Leo and Diane Dillon. New York, Dutton [1971] 47 p.   PZ8.3.J125 Gas

> Four times
>   Wagadu rose.
>   A great city, gleaming in the light of day,
> Four times
>   Wagadu fell.
>   And disappeared from human sight.
>   Once through vanity.
>   Once through dishonesty.
>   Once through greed.
>   Once through discord. . . .

Here we have a poetic rendition of "a legend from the Sudan of West Africa, which is, in its present form, at least as old as the seventeenth century." In her introduction the author notes that the legend is one of the few surviving pieces of the still earlier and greater epic, the *Dausi*. "Most of the *Dausi* has been lost . . . but it was originally a long, continuous epic that chronicled the legendary history of the Soninke . . . [and] the rise and fall of their city-state, Wagadu."

The poem tells of Gassire, a warrior prince of the ruling family who renounces his noble birth to become the first bard of the Soninke people, and of the fall of the first Wagadu.

60. Okeke, Uche.
TALES OF LAND OF DEATH: IGBO FOLKTALES, as told and illustrated by Uche Okeke. Garden City, N.Y., Zenith Books, 1971. 114 p.   PZ8.1.O4

Forty traditional Igbo tales, representing *Iro,* the spoken narrative, *Ita,* the sung, and *Iro/Ita,* a combination of both. The author states in his introduction that these "serve as a means of instructing and entertaining the audience." A dominant theme is man's relationship with the seen and unseen world. Many of the narratives have animals, such as Mbe the Tortoise, a stock hero, enacting the roles of human beings.

Riddles are included.

Somber brush paintings complement the mood of the text.

61. Robinson, Adjai.
    SINGING TALES OF AFRICA. Illustrated by Christine Price. New York, C. Scribner's Sons [1974] 80 p.   M1830.A2R6

Seven *Märchen* and animal stories are prefaced with a short introduction that describes African storytelling, pointing to the song within the tale, the "action" story which "tells itself in song and bodily motion," and audience participation. Each story, preceded by the words of its song and melody lines of music, was told to the author by his mother and grandmother when he was a child. Two of them, in which huts have rooms and Bra Spider wears a top hat and tuxedo, reflect a changing world. Animal heroes include Tortoise, Spider, and Baboon; other important characters are man-eating giants and genii. The didacticism, usually so strong in African tales, has been softened here. Notes explain the meaning of the tales.

Effective full-page woodcuts and smaller decorations.

62. Sidahome, Joseph E.
    STORIES OF THE BENIN EMPIRE. School ed. Ibadan, Oxford University Press, 1967. 132 p. illus.   PZ4.S567 St

Nine traditional tales from the Edo people as told to the author by various storytellers and put into English for use in a reader or text for students of English. They lack flavor and dramatic impact because explanatory material worked into the texts, often in the form of conversation, impedes the narrative flow, and the prose is pedestrian. However, there is interest for the researcher in the characters and plots—orphan boys, extraordinary children, magic, secret societies, and old women endowed with mysterious powers—and the picture provided of life under the Obas in the old Benin empire.

63. Sturton, Hugh.
    ZOMO, THE RABBIT; [tales] Drawings by Peter Warner.

New York, Atheneum, 1966. 128 p.   PZ7.S9413 Zo

The publisher's note at the end of this collection describes Zomo as "a disreputable but authentic character of African folklore . . . [who] originally came from Hausaland, in what is now Northern Nigeria." It states further that since literal translations are stark and many endings "bloody," the author "has felt justified in discarding the less attractive heroes and awarding their parts to Zomo, modifying some of the plots, and supplying some of the missing verbal embroidery." Thus Zomo stands forth as a less malicious and unscrupulous hero than he does in the original stories.

"The Animals' Farm" provides an example of the textual alteration, for ordinarily it is the Hare (Rabbit) who is the thief and causes an innocent dupe to be slain. "Zomo Pays His Debts" also shows a change, for usually the creditors are eaten by other creditors until there is no one left but the triumphant, wicked Hare (or other trickster). In his fluid and colloquial telling, Sturton keeps to the present tense, thus "suggesting the flavor of the original storyteller's language which has little or no past tense."

> Zomo the Rabbit is never a great one for work. He will tell you that he likes using his head, not his hands, but the truth is that unless he has to, he will not use either.
> One day his wife comes and asks him for money so that she can go and buy food. Zomo puts his hand into his right pocket and it is empty. Then he tries his left pocket and that is empty, too.
> "Oho," says his wife, "so that's how it is, is it? Very well—no money, no supper."
>   From "Zomo Pays His Debts"

Expressive animal drawings in fine line.

64. Walker, Barbara K.
   THE DANCING PALM TREE, AND OTHER NIGERIAN FOLKTALES. Woodcuts by Helen Siegl. New York, Parents' Magazine Press [1968] 112 p.   PZ8.1.W128 Dan

In a short introduction the reteller notes: "All the tales in this collection were told by Olawale Idewu, a young Nigerian student in an American college, lonesome for home and happy to share the stories that are part of his heritage." She then describes storytelling, the riddle formula, and the story itself —"as much a play and a musical performance as a story, because the storyteller really becomes a part of the story, imitating sounds and gestures, acting out what happens, singing the songs the characters sing, prostrating himself where some unfortunate fellow in the tale must humble himself before a superior."

The stories, expanded to include explanations of customs, reveal the moral code and values of the Yoruba. Thus they show that tricksters pay at last for their wiliness, an over-proud king discovers that God is more powerful than he, and a poor man learns the results of violating a taboo:

> "Go to the green door," said the king, his voice low now, and sorrowful. "Take your ragged clothes and your bundle of wood. It is not other people's good wishes which can make you happy, but your own destiny. Sell your wood, since work is the cure for poverty. But know this, my friend: your misfortune is not the fault of Adam."
>
> Iyapò arose. He walked on his bare feet past the fine shoes he had lost, past the handsome robe he had flung aside, to the green door. Opening it, he put on his ragged clothes, which scarcely covered his stout figure. Lifting the bundle of wood to his shoulders, he walked out of the cool palace into the dust and heat of the market. "Wood! Wood for sale!" he called. "Wood! Good wood for sale!" But no matter how many times he cried his "Wood for sale!" there was no longer a mention of Adam.
>
> From "It's All the Fault of Adam"

Three of the tales have appeared elsewhere: "A Lesson for Bat" (*The Instructor,* October 1965) as "Why the Bat Is Ashamed To Be Seen"; "It's All the Fault of Adam" (*Humpty Dumpty's Magazine for Little Children,* December 1965) as "Adam and the Woodcutter"; and "The Hunter and the Hind" (adapted from "The Hunter and the Deer" in Idewu's *Nigerian Folk Tales,* item 35).

A glossary supplies additional information about customs, names, and variants, e.g., the Tar Baby motif in "The Dancing Palm Tree."

Attractive full-page pictures and strip designs enhance the appearance of the volume.

Collections for Children

Woodcut by Helen Siegl from The Dancing Palm Tree, and Other Nigerian Folktales *by Barbara Walker. Item 64.*

Silk screens here and on pages 62 and 63 by Leo and Diane Dillon from Behind the Back of the Mountain; Black Folktales from Southern Africa *by Verna Aardema. Item 84.*

Southern Africa

Countries represented here are South Africa, South-West Africa, Rhodesia, Angola, Mozambique, Swaziland, Lesotho, Botswana, Zambia, and Malawi.

Noticeable in Southern African folklore are tales of marvels (or *Märchen*) with highly individual elements such as cannibals and the old wise women with sores. Also widely prevalent are the tales of human and animal tricksters—Hlakanyana, a human also called "little weasel," and Little Hare, both repellently sadistic characters. The "Hottentots" had Jackal and the "Bushmen" had Mantis, a strange figure symbolizing the ideal "Bushman."

STUDIES AND COLLECTIONS FOR ADULTS

65. Baumbach, E. J. M., *and* C. T. D. Marivate.
 XIRONGA FOLK-TALES. Illustrations by Raymond Andrews. Pretoria, University of South Africa, 1973. 197 p.
 GR360.T5B38

These 18 tales, each accompanied by its Xironga text, have been "recorded, exactly as they were told by different narrators" and translated "as far as possible . . . word for word and . . . sentence for sentence." They abound in such magic ingredients as a man snake, a python doctor, and a magic mirror. Their themes deal with laziness, greed, jealousy, famine, drought, cunning, and bravery. Humor lights up "The Thieves" (a "Bremen Town Musicians" variant), "The Hare" (a Tar Baby variant), and "The Dishonest Visitors." In the last, travelers given hospitality steal a hen and her eggs from their hosts; however, they do not leave until the chicken is cooked. While waiting, the father keeps his hosts outside talking, and when the chicken is done, the son announces the fact to his father:

 ". . . You, father,
 What will it help us to stay here any longer?
 Now, it is far to at the-chicken-is-cooked, the place where

we are going. When, then, shall we arrive there?"
And the father instructs his son as follows:
"What has gone into your head boy?
Are you mad, what has possessed you?
Do you think at drink-the-gravy-and-take-the-fowl-and-put-it-into-the-provision-basket is as far as where we are going to at the-fowl-is-cooked?" . . .
The boy got the message that his father wanted him to drink the gravy and then take the fowl and put it into the provision basket.

66. Bishop, Herbert L.
A SELECTION OF ŠIRONGA FOLKLORE. South African journal of science, v. 19, Dec. 1922: 383–400. Q85.S5, v. 19

Cycle stories about Nwampfundla the Hare told for the writer, a missionary, by Samuel Mabika, "in his youth a great warrior, a man of considerable importance in his tribe." The short, tellable narratives have an appealing dramatic quality and subtle humor. The author-translator has endeavored to be faithful to the originals, while commenting: "It is, unfortunately, impossible to reproduce the vivacity, the interpretative gesture, the free use of 'descriptive complements,' and the very evident enjoyment of the stories shown by the narrator." Other, and less attractive, forms of some of the tales appear in Rev. Henri Junod's *The Life of a South African Tribe* (item 75) and *Les Chants et les contes des Ba-Ronga* (see note for item 75).

The cycle is followed (p. 401–415) by "A Selection of ŠiRonga Proverbs" collected by the author from various sources. A very few—for example, "When water is spilt, it can no longer be gathered up"—appear to be clear parallels of European proverbs.

67. Bleek, Wilhelm H. I., *and* Lucy C. Lloyd.
THE MANTIS AND HIS FRIENDS; BUSHMAN FOLKLORE. Edited by D. F. Bleek. Illustrated with many reproductions of Bushman drawings. Cape Town, T. M. Miller [1924]
68 p. Micro 21563 GR

The reteller, a daughter of Dr. Bleek, has, without sacrificing flavor, given form and coherence to 23 stories taken from his *Specimens of Bushman Folklore* (item 69). These revolve around Mantis, an ideal "Bushman," and reflect the way he lived "over a century ago." Mantis is filled with contradictions.

He is the possessor of supernatural powers; he created the moon and other heavenly bodies; he can bring people to life. At the same time he is often extremely foolish, or mischievous, occasionally kind, and always very human.

Other characters in the narratives include Mantis' adopted daughter Porcupine, daughter of the All-Devourer; Kwammang-a, called by Mantis "my sister's son . . . a mythical person not identified with any animal but seen in the rainbow"; Kwammang-a's two children, young Kwammang-a and young Ichneuman, a great talker who often upbraids his grandfather Mantis for his foolishness. All these characters are animals though they were once men and women of "the early race."

68. Bleek, Wilhelm H. I.
REYNARD THE FOX IN SOUTH AFRICA; OR, HOTTENTOT FABLES AND TALES. Chiefly translated from original manuscripts in the library of . . . Sir George Grey. London, Trübner, 1864. xxxi, 94 p.   GR360.H7B4

Here in a collection directed to "the general public" are 13 Jackal fables, seven tales about Sun and Moon, and other narratives about Tortoise, Baboon, Lion, and Heitsi Eibip, the Namaqua sorcerer. A number of individual tales are followed by variants; there are, for example, five versions of the coming of death, including one from the Zulu. A few "Songs of Praise" have been included.

The author, a well-known 19th-century German philologist and one of the pioneer collectors of South African folklore, notes in his preface that except for a few slight omissions and alterations, necessary for English readers, the translation is faithful to the original.

69. ———, comp.
SPECIMENS OF BUSHMAN FOLKLORE. Collected by the late W. H. I. Bleek and L. C. Lloyd; edited by the latter; with an introduction by George McCall Theal. Translation into English; illustrations; and appendix. London, G. Allen, 1911. xl, 468 p. plates (part col.), ports. (part col.)
GR360.B9B4

"The original Bushman text . . . is printed side by side with the English translation."

A work consisting of native texts and their translations, designed to assist those wishing to study the San language. The materials are divided into two categories: the first, Mythology, Fables, Legends, and Poetry; the second, History (Natural and Personal). A preface by Dr. Bleek's sister-in-law comments on linguistic problems and also describes the narrators.

In his introduction George McCall Theal provides a little of Khoisan history and an account of how the texts were collected. The narratives, meticulously recorded and literally translated, are fragmentary and repetitious. Detailed footnotes accompany the texts.

70. Brownlee, Frank.
    LION AND JACKAL, WITH OTHER NATIVE FOLK TALES FROM SOUTH AFRICA. London, G. Allen & Unwin [1938] 174 p.
    GR350.B7

Twenty-nine stories categorized as Animal Stories, Cannibal Stories, Stories of Hlakanyana, Stories of Fabulous Creatures, and Miscellaneous Stories. They have been set down faithfully in words close to those in which they were related to the author, who endeavoured to keep their original simplicity. Appendix 1 consists of comment about the origin of the stories. Here the author indicates that variants of "Lion and Jackal" and "Dove and Jackal" are included in Bleek's *Reynard the Fox in South Africa* (item 68). Appendix 2, The Native's Mental Horizon, discusses culture and society.

71. Callaway, Henry, *Bp.*
    NURSERY TALES, TRADITIONS, AND HISTORIES OF THE ZULUS, IN THEIR OWN WORDS. With a translation into English, and notes. v. 1. Westport, Conn., Negro Universities Press [1970] 375 p.
    PL8844.A2C3

Reprint of the 1868 ed.

Issued in six parts, 1866–68, with title: *Izinganekwane, nensumansumane, nezindaba zabantu.*

No more published.

These thoroughly documented narratives were recorded by an English medical missionary, first Bishop of Kaffraria, who is considered to be "a hallowed name" in the history of Anglo-African folklore (Richard Dorson, *The British Folklorists; a History*, p. 353; see item 2). The author carefully indicates the relationships of these tales to those of Europe and elsewhere, thus making his collection valuable to the student of comparative literature.

Among the stories is the "History of the Travels and Adventures of Uthlakanyana" ("a kind of Tom Thumb, the Giant Killer"), whose malicious cunning is exerted on his father, mother, and all whom he encounters. The story is closely akin to the Xhosa tale "Hlakanyana" and also to stories of Hare and Jackal. Among the stories most likely to appeal to children, if adapted, are "Ukcombekcantsini," about a boy and girl magically born to a childless queen; "Umkxakaza-wakoginqwayo," a princess carried off by a magical beast who "seem[ed] a moving land"; and "Umdhlubu and the Frog," about a princess who was rescued by a frog. Another attractive story, "Ubongopa-kamagadhela," about a boy with magical skills and his wonderful ox, has been retold by Phyllis Savory in her *Zulu Fireside Tales* as "The Love of Kevelinda" (see item 17).

Further discussion of Zulu folklore may be found in chapter 6 of Eileen Krige's *The Social System of the Zulus* (London, Longmans, Green [1936] 420 p. DT878.Z9K7). Here the author provides additional insight into the story of Uhlakanyana (Uthlakanyana), the dwarf, very like a weasel in that he is cunning and a "trouble to man," despised by his people whom he constantly deceives. She also comments on fantastic animals like the Imbulu, on "foreign motifs," prevalent themes, and types of Zulu tales.

72. Chatelain, Héli.
FOLK-TALES OF ANGOLA. FIFTY TALES, WITH KI-MBUNDU TEXT, LITERAL ENGLISH TRANSLATION, INTRODUCTION, AND NOTES. New York, Negro Universities Press [1969, c1894] 315 p. maps.   GR360.A5C3 1969

Bibliography: p. 310.

A work intended to be a textbook for students of the language and comparative literature. In preliminary matter, which consists of an introduction to the country, people, and language, the author devotes a chapter to African folklore, its classification, and the work of the famous 19th-century collectors. Each genre is described in brief. The author comments on symbolism in the animal world: the elephant expressing wisdom and strength, the hyena, brute force and stupidity. His comparative notes indicate the relationship of black American folklore to the African, inter-African resemblances, and the influence of Portuguese and Italian traditions.

The tales in this collection represent the *mi-soso* ("fictitious" stories or *Märchen*) and *maka* ("records of events").

73. Honeij, James A.
SOUTH AFRICAN FOLK TALES. New York, Negro Universities Press [1969] 151 p.   GR350.H5 1969
Reprint of the 1910 ed.

Bibliography: p. 148–151.

A collection of animal stories, cited among works considered "les plus importants" by Veronika Görög-Karady in her *Littérature orale africaine* (item 3).

Many of the tales appeared in pre-1880 English collections; others are taken from Dutch sources; and a few are retold from memory: ". . . in all cases they are as nearly like the original as a translation from one tongue to another will allow." The majority come from the "Bushmen"; others are "perverted types . . . [which] have been taken over by Hottentots or Zulus." These latter reflect a European influence, as in "The World's Reward," a tale similar to "The Bremen Town Musicians." In some, akin to stories of Brer Rabbit or African Hare, Jackal plays the role of chief protagonist.

A number of the tales appeared first under Honeij's name in American magazines, "but this is the first time [1910] that a complete collection has appeared since Dr. Bleek published his stories in 1864." The author has limited the compilation to animal stories and fables, excluding any with a mythological or religious significance. For some of the tales variants are included.

74. Jacottet, Édouard, *ed. and tr.*
THE TREASURY OF BA-SUTO LORE; BEING ORIGINAL SE-SUTO TEXTS, with a literal English translation and notes, published under the direction of E. Jacottet. v. 1. Morija, Basutoland (South Africa), Sesuto Book Depot; London, K. Paul, Trench, Trübner, 1908. xxviii, 287 p.
                                 Micro 19977 GR

"A list of the most important books dealing with South African or Bantu folk-lore, or to which reference is made in the notes": p. 286–287.

In his introduction to this rich collection, the author, a

French missionary, comments on a "similarity of thought and structure" in the folktale the world over, the work of other collectors, and African folklore and its distribution. Sotho tales fall into three groups—*Märchen,* the most numerous; animal stories; and moral, or household, tales. In speaking of the animal stories, he notes the likeness of Hare, "the cunning animal par excellence," to Fox in Europe and points out that the role of Hare is taken by a human trickster, Uhlakanyana (the weasel), in Zulu folklore.

Notes to the tales refer mainly to "Bantu" and South African folktales.

Here is a part of "The Child With a Moon on His Breast":

> It is said that there was a great chief called Bulane. He had two wives. One of them had no children, but the other had. The chief had a moon on his breast. One of the wives was greatly loved by Bulane; she was the one who had children. She used to torment the one who had no children.
>
> After a while, the childless one became pregnant. The months went by, and the time arrived when she was confined. Now the wife who had children came to help her. The woman gave birth to a child who had a moon on his breast. The woman who acted as midwife took the child, and threw him away under the pots in the back part of the hut. A mouse took him quickly. . . .

Another important work translated by the author from Sotho into his native French is *Contes populaires des Bassoutos (Afrique du Sud)* (Paris, E. Leroux, 1895. 292 p. Collection de contes et chansons populaires, 20. GR15.C6, no. 20).

75. Junod, Henri A.
THE LIFE OF A SOUTH AFRICAN TRIBE. New Hyde Park, N.Y., University Books [1962] 2 v. illus., ports., map.

GN657.T5J82

A Swiss missionary's detailed study of the Thonga peoples of Mozambique. First published in 1912 and reissued in a revised and enlarged edition in 1927, the present volume is "a complete reproduction" of that edition. Thonga social life—"its customs in relation to the individual, communal and national life"—is described in volume 1. Volume 2 examines Thonga "Mental and Spiritual Life, its Literature and Music, its Religion, Magic and Morality." Pages 176–275 here concern the "three different styles" of folklore: proverbs and riddles, poetry (lyric, epic, satiric, and the like), and tales. Discussed in relation to the role they play in the life of the people, and their literary, ethnographic, moral, and philosophical values, the tales are classified as follows: animal folktales (stories of Hare, Tortoise, and Small Toad as tricksters); ". . . stories in which human beings, children, the miserable and despised, triumph over their elders and those who hate them"; Ogre tales; moral tales; tales based on "more or less historic" fact; and foreign tales, "which have come from Moslem, Portuguese, or English sources, but have been altered in a very curious way, thus affording interesting material for the study of the Native mind." Texts of 11 narratives are included.

More selections in the above categories are to be found in the author's *Les Chants et les contes des Ba-Ronga de la baie de Delagoa* (Lausanne, Switzerland, G. Bridel [1897] 327 p. GR360.T5J8).

76. Kidd, Dudley.
THE ESSENTIAL KAFIR. With sixty-three full-page illustrations from photographs by the author. Freeport, N.Y., Books for Libraries Press [1971] xiv, 435 p.
DT764.X6K5 1971
"First published 1904."
Bibliography: p. 417-428.

Thirteen Xhosa narratives, with an appendix which discusses Heitsi-Eibib, a mythical hero of the "Hottentots" and "Bushmen." The author also lists here 20 components from which African storytellers have created their "thousands of permutations and combinations," such as birds capable of producing milk, empty huts (indicating cannibals), and abnormal births. Melodies for a few songs have been supplied. Three of the stories may be found also in the author's book for young readers, *The Bull of the Kraal and the Heavenly Maidens; a Tale of Black Children* (item 88).

77. ———.
SAVAGE CHILDHOOD; A STUDY OF KAFIR CHILDREN. New York, Negro Universities Press [1969] xiv, 314 p. illus., music.
GN482.K4 1969
Reprint of the 1906 ed.

Studies and Collections for Adults 59

In this study of Xhosa childhood the writer has supplied a selection of "surprise stories," or nursery tales, which are literal translations of the narratives of the "natives" and thus here retain their storytelling quality. The animal stories, a number of which resemble those of the Zulu, include a few of the Brer Rabbit genre, while "The Lion and the Gazelle," as the author points out, is "wonderfully similar in moral" to the Persian "Camel and the Miller." Among others with a particular appeal for children are "How Skin-Sore Killed a Cannibal," "The Man Who Hid His Honey," and "The Child in the Drum."

78. Markowitz, Arthur.
WITH UPLIFTED TONGUE: STORIES, MYTHS AND FABLES OF THE SOUTH AFRICAN BUSHMEN, TOLD IN THEIR MANNER. Illustrated by Arthur Goldreich. [Johannesburg] Central News Agency [1957?] 77 p.   GR360.B9M37

A readable presentation of 35 narratives and poems, without the "endless repetitions and digressions" inherent in the "Bushman" style of narration. The author has "restricted himself to the Bushman vocabulary" and, by trying to avoid "sacrificing too much of their elliptical style," has preserved their primitive appeal. Thus the stories have a unity and coherence lacking in scholarly translations by such eminent authorities as Dr. Wilhelm Bleek.

A number of the stories—"The Little Hare," "The Rebirth of the Ostrich," "The Woman Who Was a Sister to Vultures," "The Thunderstorm," "How a Bad Girl Was Punished," "The Young Man Who Was Carried Off by a Lion," and "When Kagara and Chaunu Fight Each Other"—have potential interest for children.

79. Martin, Minnie.
BASUTOLAND; ITS LEGENDS AND CUSTOMS. New York, Negro Universities Press [1969] 174 p.   DT786.M3 1969
Reprint of the 1903 ed.

The author, wife of a government official, has included 10 Sotho narratives in her short account of the history of Lesotho (formerly Basutoland), beginning with the middle of the 18th century. They describe famine, a bird that gives milk, cannibals, giants, and men turned into snakes.

The writer has also prepared a work for children, *Tales of the African Wilds,* 2d ed. (Cape Town, Maskew Miller [1969] 93 p. PZ8.2.M35 Tal 3), which is marred by a coyness that robs the material of its intrinsic appeal.

80. Postma, Minnie, *comp.*
    TALES FROM THE BASOTHO. Translated from Afrikaans by Susie McDermid. Analytical notes, tale type and motif indexes by John M. Vlack. Austin, Published for the American Folklore Society by the University of Texas Press [1974] xxv, 177 p. illus. (Publication of the American Folklore Society. Memoir series, v. 59)
    GR360.B3P613

Translation of *Litsōmo.*

Bibliography: p. 175–177.

> "Good morning, mother of mine," Jackal greeted her.
> "Yes, I greet you," she replied.
> "Are you still living?" he asked, according to the correct way in which one person greets another.
> "Yes, I am still living. And you? Are you still living also?"
> "Yes, I too am still living, Mother," he replied. And then he asked, as the custom was, "Did you wake well this morning?"
>
> From "The Jackal and Hen"

Repetition of words, use of idiomatic phrases ("her heart was black" and "her heart did not want to lie down"), African ideophones *(tsoko, tsoko, tsoko* for the sound of the whirlwind), and such distinctive endings as *"Ke tsomo ka mathetho* . . . this is a true tale of the Basotho people" impart authenticity and color to these narratives and reflect something of the style of the originals. The stories make a rich source for the reteller—about animals, man-eaters, half-people, great snakes, and monsters such as the nanabolele "who give off light in the dark, as the moon and the stars give off light in the dark."

In addition to motif and tale type indexes, the appendix includes a listing of tale types under "Comparable African Folktales."

81. Stayt, Hugh A.
    THE BAVENDA. [London] F. Cass, 1968. xviii, 392 p. illus., map, music, plates (part fold.), ports. (Cass library of

African studies. General studies, no. 58)

GN657.B3S7 1968

Reprint of 1931 ed.

Bibliography: p. [377]-379.

Chapter 24 in this study of the Venda culture in South Africa concerns folklore and includes 16 texts for animal stories, *Märchen,* and trickster tales. Some of them, such as "The Chief With the Half-moon on His Chest," "How All the Animals Got Their Color," and "How Animals Got Their Tails," are clearly of interest to children.

Songs and their scores are provided for the first three tales, illustrating how they are circulated among the people.

82. Theal, George M.
KAFFIR FOLK-LORE: A SELECTION FROM THE TRADITIONAL TALES CURRENT AMONG THE PEOPLE LIVING ON THE EASTERN BORDER OF THE CAPE COLONY, WITH COPIOUS EXPLANATORY NOTES. Westport, Conn., Negro Universities Press [1970] 226 p.   GR360.K2T3 1970

Reprint of the 1886 ed.

Tales collected by a former mission teacher and border magistrate from the Xhosa people.

The introductory material provides insight into the life and culture of the Xhosa: their relationship with the "Hottentots," customs, methods of government, physical appearance, language, and religious beliefs—in the Supreme Being called Quamata and in an unseen world peopled by water sprites, hobgoblins, and other malevolent spirits.

The tales represent only a small portion of Xhosa folklore. Many are so constructed that they are "capable of almost indefinite expansion . . . [since] parts of one can be made to fit into parts of another, so as to form a new tale." Among the selections are "The Story of Hlakanyana," "the little deceiver" who resembles the European Tom Thumb in stature only; "Story of the Wonderful Horns," akin to "Billy Beg and His Bull"; "Story of the Hare," and "Story of Lion and Little Jackal." A number of tales contain song lyrics. A listing, with explanation, of some of the most common proverbs, "figurative expressions," and ethnographic notes about individual stories conclude the volume.

Most of these tales may be found in the next item.

83. ———.
THE YELLOW AND DARK-SKINNED PEOPLE OF AFRICA SOUTH OF THE ZAMBESI. A description of the Bushmen, the Hottentots, and particularly the Bantu, with 15 plates and numerous folklore tales of these different people. New York, Negro Universities Press [1969] xvi, 397 p. illus., ports. DT737.T48 1969

Reprint of the 1910 ed.

Four chapters in this historical and ethnographical study of the Khoisan ("Bushmen" and "Hottentots") and Xhosa peoples contain traditional tales. In the trickster stories Jackal, or Little Jackal, is the animal antihero, and Hlakanyana (Little Deceiver) is the human antihero. Other story types are myths and fables. The "Bantu" stories have been taken from the item above.

COLLECTIONS FOR CHILDREN

84. Aardema, Verna.
BEHIND THE BACK OF THE MOUNTAIN; BLACK FOLKTALES FROM SOUTHERN AFRICA. Retold by Verna Aardema. Pictures by Leo and Diane Dillon. New York, Dial Press [1973] 85 p.   PZ8.1.A213 Be

In a style suitable for storytelling the author has retold 10 appealing stories from Southern African traditions. The language is direct and suggestive of the spareness of the originals. In most instances the reteller has kept close to her sources. "Little Hen Eagle" (based on the complex "Untombi-Yapansi" in Callaway's *Nursery Tales, Traditions, and Histories of the Zulus,* item 71) has had more alteration, with characters and

incidents omitted. However, the spirit of the original narrative has been preserved here, as well. The silk-screen pictures add to the distinction of the work.
A bibliography of sources and a glossary are appended.

85. Bourhill, Mrs. E. J., and Mrs. J. B. Drake.
    FAIRY TALES FROM SOUTH AFRICA. Collected from original native sources. With illustrations by W. Herbert Holloway. London, Macmillan, 1908. xv, 249 p.   PZ8.B6444 Fai

A 1973 reprint has been issued by the Books for Libraries Press, Freeport, N.Y.

Twenty tales, taken primarily from Swazi sources but including a small representation from other Southern African peoples, have been retold for children by two Englishwomen in a mildly condescending style, characteristic of the period. The stories are filled with princesses and princes, magic, supernatural beings, and "half people." Songs without melodies are included in the text.

Ten of the tales have been adapted in Terry Berger's *Black Fairy Tales*, with drawings by David Omar White (New York, Atheneum, 1969. 137 p. PZ8.B449 Bl). In this volume are an occasional unnecessary softening of the earlier text and gratuitous use of the descriptive word "black."

86. Helfman, Elizabeth S.
    THE BUSHMEN AND THEIR STORIES. Drawings by Richard Cuffari. New York, Seabury Press [1971] 128 p.
    PZ8.1.H378 Bu

Most of the 17 retellings published here for children have been taken from translations of Dr. Wilhelm H. I. Bleek; "though they have been kept as close as possible to the feeling and style of the original, [they] have been simplified and partly rewritten." Comment on the San philosophy and way of life is included in the text; the whole is more useful for the study of Africa than for storytelling.

Graphically illustrated with many line-and-wash drawings.

87. Hertslet, Jessie.
    BANTU FOLK TALES, SEVEN STORIES. Lino-cut illustrations by Joyce Wallis. Cape Town, African Bookman, 1946. 91 p.
    GR360.B2H37

Collections for Children

Adaptations of stories from Callaway's *Nursery Tales, Traditions and Histories of the Zulus* (item 71), Theal's *The Yellow and Dark-Skinned People of Africa* (item 83), *Folklore Journal*, September 1880, and *uHlabanengalwi*, by A. H. S. Mbata and G. C. S. Mdhladhla (Durban, T. W. Griggs, 1946. 108 p. illus. PL8844.M37U35). The tales present a child nurtured by the waves and later raised by cannibals, a dumb boy mysteriously restored to speech, maidens turned into birds, a chief's arrogant daughter, a girl who became a child of the moon, and Kenkebe, the Greedy.

These stories are not only pleasing in content and style, but they are also offered in an elegantly produced volume, with lino-cuts and text printed in sepia.

88. Kidd, Dudley.
 THE BULL OF THE KRAAL AND THE HEAVENLY MAIDENS; A TALE OF BLACK CHILDREN. London, A. and C. Black, 1908. 302 p. illus., 12 col. plates.   PZ7.K53 Bu

Eleven traditional Xhosa nursery tales and nursery rhymes are interwoven in a story about the life of a chief's little son. Seven of the stories concern a young man with skin sores—a recurring figure in African folklore—and others deal with animals. There is also a variant of "The Child in the Drum." A few of the stories contain chants.

"How Skin-Sore Killed a Cannibal," "The Man, the Lion, and the Mouse," and "The Child in the Drum" may also be located in the author's *Savage Childhood* (item 77).

89. Leshoai, Benjamin L.
 MASILO'S ADVENTURES, AND OTHER STORIES. [London] Longmans [1968] 65 p. illus.   GR360.L4L4

Four Sotho narratives "told the author as a child by his grandmother in the evening outside her mudhouse." These have been somewhat embellished to provide background for his children and "the coming generations," and thus lack true storytelling quality. Two of the stories tell of the giant Limo; one describes "the fearful Kholumolumo," a monster, and the other a Mosel'antga, an evil creature similar to the Zulu imbulu. A brief introduction comments on the traditional Sotho story.

From The Lion on the Path, and Other African Stories *by Hugh Tracey, illustrated by Eric Byrd. Item 90.*

90. Tracey, Hugh.
    THE LION ON THE PATH, AND OTHER AFRICAN STORIES. With illustrations by Eric Byrd and music transcribed by Andrew Tracey. New York, Praeger [1968, c1967] xiv, 127 p.   PZ8.1.T64 Li 3

First published in London.

" . . . the only collection of African folklore [for children] which approaches being truly African both in content and style" (Nancy J. Schmidt, "Collections of African Folklore for Children," in *Research in African Literatures*, v. 2, fall 1971, p. 150–167. See item 7.).

The 25 tales, collected by a musicologist, have been recorded from Shona and South African storytellers and are largely about "the other folk of the countryside," animal characters who meet and talk with men as equals. Two stories, "Chief Above and Chief Below" and "Kamiyo of the River," resemble the Greek myths about Persephone and

Pygmalion. Another, "Rabbit at the Water Hole," is akin to the Tar Baby tales.

The stories are designed for telling, "preferably from memory." The traditional African narrative style used throughout has preserved the formula beginnings and endings, original idioms, and repetitions of "and's," "now's," and "so's," as well as African names, words, songs, and music.

A foreword supplies the background for the stories and explains symbolic roles played by the animals. Instructions for the storyteller, with a description of African storytelling, are also provided.

Five of the tales have been recorded by Mr. Tracey on a phonodisc entitled *African Stories Told by Hugh Tracey* (Decca LF 1174. [195–] 2 s. 10 in. 33 1/3 rpm. microgroove. Music of Africa series, no. 9).

From The Lion on the Path. *Item 90.*

Central Africa

Included here are Chad, Central African Republic, Zaire, Congo People's Republic, Gabon, Cameroon, Rwanda, Burundi, and Equatorial Guinea.

Instructive as well as entertaining, the tales tell of animals and of everyday life. The latter describe hunting and other adventures in the bush, greedy parents, in-laws, and the unfaithful wife. Among the stock characters in the Congolese basin are Tshikashi Tshikulu, an old woman endowed with strange powers who lives in the forest, and the tricksters—Hare, sometimes called Kalulu; Tortoise; and Kabuluku, the little antelope.

STUDIES AND COLLECTIONS FOR ADULTS

91. Burton, William F. P.
    THE MAGIC DRUM; TALES FROM CENTRAL AFRICA. Illustrated by Ralph Thompson. New York, Criterion [1962, c1961] 127 p. (A Criterion book for young people)
    PZ8.B944 Mag 2

In his preface the author describes the "most accurate and efficient teaching system" followed by the people of the Congo —one that "fits a native for adult life and is the product of the needs of the Central African environment and the demands of Central African youth." He discusses the role in this of the *bamfumu* (counselors of a chief), who often have their own specialties: "the *balute,* or 'men of memory' as the village historians love to be called, can go back over two or three centuries of Luban history." Other elders have an inexhaustible store of proverbs, maxims, and fables. The 72 examples given here (as well known among the Luba as Cinderella in western culture) have served through centuries to coach the young in "various modes of social intercourse." The author concludes by expressing his regret that their natural beauties are lost in "our stereotyped cut-and-dried English. . . . To be heard at their best, the fables must be told by the old, half-naked Luban *bamfumu* through the smoke of a village fire, with the dark forest trees as a background, and to the accompaniment of chirping crickets, the croaking of frogs in the stream, and the distant call of the jackal and the hyena."

Most of the narratives tell about animals—Rabbit, Bushbuck, Leopard, Squirrel, Elephant, and Tortoise—in human roles, with a full measure of human foibles. A number are trickster tales. Others point out the consequences of greed, jealousy, laziness, vanity, and rudeness. Some are parallels of familiar stories: "Two Wild Ducks and a Tortoise" ("The Talkative Tortoise"), "The Tortoise and the Reed-buck Run a Race" ("The Hare and the Tortoise"), and "The Friendship of the Hippo, the Crocodile and the Baboon" ("The Monkey and the Crocodile"). Elements of "Ali Baba and the Forty Thieves" are found in "The Rabbit Shows the Bushbuck a New Way of Hunting." "The Two Boxes," of more recent vintage, accounts for differences between white men and black men.

Illustrated with small, lively sketches in ink line.

92. Dennett, Richard E.
NOTES ON THE FOLK-LORE OF THE FJORT (FRENCH CONGO). With an introduction by Mary H. Kingsley. London, Published for the Folk-Lore Society by D. Nutt, 1898. xxxii, 169 p. plates. (Publications of the Folk-Lore Society, 41) GR360.B18D4

Perhaps it may interest you to know how a story is told.
Imagine, then, a village in a grove of graceful palm trees. The full moon is shining brightly upon a small crowd of Negroes seated round a fire in an open space in the centre of the village. One of them has just told a story, and his delighted audience demands another. Thus he begins:
"Let us tell another story; let us be off!"
All then shout: "Pull away!"
"Let us be off!" he repeats.
And they answer again: "Pull away!"
Then the storyteller commences: "There were two brothers, the Smart Man and the Fool."

Thirty-three "legal," historical, and "play" stories gathered by the author, a British trader, who spent a number of years living with the Fjort. In her introduction, Mary H. Kingsley describes the West African scene, the relationship of the West

African to the white missionary and trader, and the "school of fetish called Nkissism" and devotes a few brief remarks to African "native" literature.

In the first two chapters the author discusses the Fjort belief in *Nkissi nsi,* "the mysterious spirit that dwells in the earth," as well as charms, taboos, customs, legends, and the manner of storytelling. His selection of tales is varied and includes a Tar Baby version entitled "The Rabbit and the Antelope." Songs are interspersed throughout the text.

Additional information about Nzambi, "the Spirit of the Earth or Old Mother Earth," Nkissism, fetishes, and songs is provided in the appendixes. Latin is employed in the translation of indelicate passages.

93. Doke, Clement M.
LAMBA FOLK-LORE. New York, American Folk-Lore Society, G. E. Stechert, Agents, 1927. xvi (i.e. xvii), 570 p. (Memoirs of the American Folk-Lore Society, v. 20)
GR1.A5, v. 20

Lamba texts and English translations.

A vast collection of tales, aphorisms, riddles, and songs from Northern Rhodesia and the Congo basin. Introducing them, the author discusses relationships between the stories and the songs, riddles, and proverbs, noting that the first often "amplify or elucidate" the others. He speaks of the "fundamental" tale, i.e., stories in which plots are almost identical although settings and characters may be different. Further, he comments on storytelling and his arrangement here of four groups of stories: animal tales (chiefly about Mr. Little-Hare, "the most cunning of all the animals . . . [who] outwits all except the Tortoise"); stories of village life (adventures in the bush, of in-laws, chiefs, and greedy parents); fairytales (beautiful princesses and fabulous wealth—both of which disappear when a taboo is violated); and ogres and gnomes. He includes 10 "choric" stories, or "prose" stories with songs, which are "mostly recited by the women and the girls, the verse parts being chanted."

The volume is a source for the researcher and reteller, although much of the material is not for children.

The songs, proverbs, and riddles are arranged alphabetically; all, stories included, are numbered.

94. Knappert, Jan.
MYTHS & LEGENDS OF THE CONGO. Nairobi, Heinemann Educational Books [1971] xiv, 218 p. (African writers series, 83)   GR360.C6K6 1971

Selections from the history, oral literature, and traditions of 10 peoples are arranged in chapters. Prefatory interpretations are supplied when necessary. The author notes the lack of knowledge of the mythology of many peoples in the Congo basin, storytelling styles, and his own method of presentation: "A straight translation of . . . these tales, either from the original language, or from the Flemish (or occasionally French) as given in a journal or learned work, has not been possible. . . . It has therefore been thought that readers who are interested in folk-lore and mythology . . . would appreciate the material better if it were rearranged to some extent. What was implied in the narrative has been made explicit, what was taken for granted has been explained. Obscure passages have been interpreted."

The tales and legends—some erotic or earthy—deal with snakes, bird spirits, the underworld, witchcraft, old hags who remove their arms and legs and roll after their victims, and cannibalism. Animals play human roles in many instances.

A useful source for the scholar.

95. Stanley, *Sir* Henry Morton.
MY DARK COMPANIONS AND THEIR STRANGE STORIES. New York, C. Scribner's Sons, 1893. 319 p. illus.   GR350.S6

The explorer-author has selected 20 Congolese tales, "the choicest and most curious of those that were related to . . . [him] during seventeen years, and which have not been hitherto published in any of my books of travel." They include a myth, "The Creation of Man"; a legend, "How Kimyera Became King of Uganda"; a story of a woman who survived alone in the bush, "The Queen of the Pool"; as well as "The Story of the Prince Who Insisted on Possessing the Moon" and a number of animal stories. These have been rendered in a style akin to that of Henry R. Schoolcraft in his collections of American Indian lore:

> Now open your ears! A huge and sour-tempered elephant went and wandered in the forest. His inside was slack for want of juicy roots and succulent reeds, but his head was as full of dark thoughts as a gadfly is full of blood. As he looked this way and that, he observed a young lion asleep

at the foot of a tree. He regarded him for a while, then, as he was in a wicked mood, it came to him that he might as well kill the lion, and he accordingly rushed forward and impaled him with his tusks. He then lifted the body with his trunk, swung it about, and dashed it against the tree, and afterwards kneeled on it until it became as shapeless as a crushed banana pulp. He then laughed and said, "Ha! ha! This is a proof that I am strong. I have killed a lion, and people will say proud things of me, and will wonder at my strength."

From "The Elephant and the Lion"

96. Torrend, J., comp.
SPECIMENS OF BANTU FOLK-LORE FROM NORTHERN RHODESIA. Texts (collected with the help of the phonograph) and English translations by J. Torrend. New York, Negro Universities Press [1969] 187 p. map.   PL8025.T6 1969

Reprint of the 1921 ed.

It consists of 25 *cante-fables,* each in their original language, accompanied by English translation and notes.

Some of the tales are allegories. "I Am Calling You Loud" —about a crocodile who lures young girls to their deaths— was used as a warning against the kidnaper who enticed young girls away, only to sell them in the slave market. Other tales relate to punishments for such crimes as murder of a wife or a child by a husband or a father. After death the victim takes the shape of a little bird and exposes the criminal. A Pygmalion type of story tells of a man who made a beautiful wife from a block of wood only to have her stolen.

Father Torrend points out that in many animal tales the creatures are treated as if they were people, and the people as animals. He notes that the mysterious little old women who appear are like fairies, workers of either good or ill. "Every tale . . . is a lesson, it may be of a principle of law, or of civilized manners . . . , or even of religious dogma, as in our tale 'Nyseyandi'; but a lesson it is, though generally hidden under a legendary or an allegorical form which rubs off anything in the shape of personal application and irritation."

97. Vyas, Chiman L.
FOLKTALES OF ZAMBIA. [Lusaka, Unity Press, 1969] 72 p.
GR360.Z275V9

The tales in this collection, as the author notes in his preface, were recorded in villages and later translated "with the help of translators in Lusaka." Since the originals were lost during Zambia's struggles for independence, the texts have been reconstructed from "the stray translation" to stimulate an interest in traditional lore and storytelling. Here are creation stories, how and why stories, hunting stories, and *Märchen*. In "The Spear Brought Fire," fire is brought to the earth from the underworld by a carpenter who journeyed there to retrieve the spear of his blacksmith brother. "The Hare and the Tortoise" appears as "Thus Failed the Rhinoceros." In two trickster stories, "Plight of Might" and "Use of Brain," Hare succeeds where mighty ones have failed, thus winning a chief's daughter. "The Bell Bewildered the Lion" resembles "Belling the Cat." In spite of stark and sometimes awkward presentation, the tales are of interest for their plots.

98. Weeks, John H.
    CONGO LIFE AND FOLKLORE; PART I, LIFE ON THE CONGO AS DESCRIBED BY A BRASS ROD; PART II, THIRTY-THREE NATIVE STORIES AS TOLD ROUND THE EVENING FIRES. London, Religious Tract Society, 1911. xxii, 468 p. illus., plates, port.
    DT650.W4

A missionary's work written "to lay clearly before the reader the ingrained prejudices, the curious views, the tremendous and all-pervading superstitions, and the mighty forces that have been arrayed against the introduction of Christianity."

In his introduction to the second part, Weeks points out that "there is, as a rule, this marked difference [between narratives told in the Upper Congo and those told in the Lower Congo]: . . . The former are explanatory of habits and customs, and the latter contain the wit, the wisdom and the moral teaching of many generations." The tales here come from the Lower Congo, written down for the author by teachers and students in a mission school. Thus they "are genuinely native in plot, situation, explanation and 'teaching,' and, wherever possible, in idiom also."

Most of the stories are about animals enacting the role of humans, with small animals (the gazelle, the squirrel, and the frog) usually overcoming larger ones. Similarities to the Brer Rabbit stories are noted. In addition there are some "puzzle" or dilemma stories—those which end in questions about who has the greatest skill. A few, like "The Son Who Tried To

Collections for Children

Woodcut by Rocco Negri from Virginia Holladay's Bantu Tales, *edited by Louise Crane. Item 101.*

Outwit His Father," are humorous and would appeal to children. The familiar tug-of-war story is here as "How the Sparrow Set the Elephant and the Crocodile To Pull Against Each Other." A Tar Baby variant appears in "The Leopard Sticks to the *Nikondi.*"

Four other animal stories are included in chapter 12, "Native Amusements," in the author's *Among the Primitive Bakongo; a Record of Thirty Years' Close Intercourse With the Bakongo and Other Tribes of Equatorial Africa, With a Description of Their Habits, Customs & Religious Beliefs* (New York, Negro Universities Press [1969] 318 p. DT650.W35 1969), a work which "aims at giving a reflection of the Lower Congo native's mind."

COLLECTIONS FOR CHILDREN

99. Chadwick, Mara L. P., *and* Louise Lamprey.
    THE ALO MAN; STORIES FROM THE CONGO. Illustrated by Rollin Crampton. Yonkers-on-Hudson, N.Y., World Book Co., 1921. 170 p.   PZ9.C21 Al

Eleven village tales interwoven with a day-to-day account of the activities of a Congolese boy and girl, Mpoko and Nkunda.

Told at night by the Alo Man, a wandering storyteller, they are chiefly about animals. A few explain animal relationships; others comment on human behavior through the activities of animals. "The String of Beads," which tells of a youngest sister endangered by a giant because of her sisters' jealousy, is a most appealing fairytale.

100. Cobble, Alice D.
WEMBI, THE SINGER OF STORIES. Illustrated by Doris Hallas. St. Louis, Bethany Press [1959] 128 p.   PZ8.1.C628 We

In her foreword the author comments: "Though these African fables are 'sung' here . . . by only one man, . . . they were really told and retold to us by countless numbers of Africans. Some were told patiently, sentence by sentence, at a time when we were not too familiar with their speech; later, others were brought in by a few of the students who heard that we were interested; still others were recounted to my husband as he spent many, many long evenings out in the villages, far away from civilization." She notes further that no two narrators told "the same story the same way" and that she has selected those which are "the most African in their narrating." However, the 25 tales, framed in a village setting where an old man tells them to children so that they may take them to their teacher at the mission school, have been "englished," becoming too wordy:

> You all know what an Antelope is. Such a fine creature of the forest! So dainty! Such slender legs! Such beautiful eyes! All the animals in the forest think the Antelope is one of the loveliest things in the world.
> None of us forget what a Spider looks like. He is very ugly, with his eight legs and his funny body. None of us like the Spider. . . .
> From "The Antelope and the Spider"

A description of a village activity precedes each story, occasionally revealing the impact of changing times upon traditional ways. Most are gently didactic. They include a dilemma tale and a number of trickster stories with Tortoise as hero. The familiar "Tug of War" appears as "The Turtle, the Hippo, and the Elephant." There is local color in African expressions and such proverbs as " '*Talobokake mpoke ea josa nd 'elok'ea mpoke e'aeyoko*' (which means: Don't throw away the old used pot—which you know—for a new one—which you don't know)."

Collections for Children 77

From Bantu Tales. *Item 101.*

101. Holladay, Virginia.
BANTU TALES. Edited by Louise Crane. Woodcuts by Rocco Negri. New York, Viking Press [1970] 95 p.
PZ8.1.H743 Ban

Nineteen *nsumuinu* (tales) from the Baluba and Lulua peoples written down in English for the author, a missionary teacher, by her American pupils who were children of missionaries. Representing *Märchen,* animal stories, and stories of everyday life, they tell of the forest; hunters; chiefs; Tshikashi Tshikulu, the old woman of the forest, sometimes kind, sometimes not; cannibals; little people; and a seven-headed giant. Kabuluku the Antelope and Nkashama the Leopard are important among the animals in the stories. Songs, African names (a pronunciation guide is appended), and expressions such as "they caught friendship" add to the flavor of the texts. Familiar themes include a child imprisoned in a drum ("The Cannibal's Drum"), the outwitting of the strong by the weak ("The Leopard and the Antelope"), and, in "The Worthless Man of Poverty," the consequences of violating a taboo:

There was once a man who was so poor that he was the talk of all the village. He had no wife, no children, no house, no manioc fields, not even a hoe. He had only a little loin cloth made of rat skins sewed together, and a pot of glue, made from sap that he had gathered in the forest, to make bird traps. Every day he would go into the forest and catch a few birds or rats so that hunger would not bite too hard. He was very happy while he was in the forest, but he had to return to the village to cook his meat. No sooner would he enter the village than all the children would come to meet him, dancing and jumping, throwing clods of dirt at him, and shouting his name with much laughter.

"Tshilandalanda wa Buhele, Luesu lua Budimba, Tuseba ku Nyima Tuseba ku Mpala, Tshilanda wa Buhele." For that was the name of reproach the village had given him, and it means "Worthless Man of Poverty, Who Has Only a Pot of Glue, and Rat Skins to Wear Fore and Aft."

Rocco Negri's striking woodcuts add to the attractiveness of the work.

102. Lantum, Daniel, *comp*.
TALES OF NSO. Illustrated by J. Jarvies. Lagos, African Universities Press [1969] 79 p. (African reader's library no. 17)   GR360.N75L36

Twelve animal stories and *Märchen* from Cameroon collected by members of the Nso Historical Society. Five, which revolve around a wily trickster, Wanyeto the Ant-eater, resemble tales told about Hare, Spider, and Tortoise. Others tell of such wonders as talking birds, an ogress, and a water spirit. "Kpuntir the Rat Hunter," a cumulative tale about a boy and his series of exchanges of possessions, differs from others of this genre in that the lad ends up emptyhanded:

"My goats and chickens! The presents the people gave me when I tricked them with the corpse; the corpse which the mourners gave me when they burst my skin on their drum; the skin the hunters gave me when they ate all my foofoo; the foofoo the baby-minders gave me when they ate all my birds; the birds which the trappers gave me when they used all my termites; the termites the diggers gave me when they broke my hoe; the hoe my father gave me when he lost my rat; the rat which I had trouble catching. Now again I have nothing. All this travelling! All this work! I am a fool!"

Although explanatory details worked into the narratives have robbed them of their storytelling qualities, the tales have potential appeal for children.

103. Savory, Phyllis.
CONGO FIRESIDE TALES. Illustrated by Joshua Tolford. New York, Hastings House [1962] 88 p. (*Her* Fireside tales series)   GR360.C6S3

In a prefatory note the author provides a description of the tales, their equatorial setting, and their folklore ingredients. She states no sources but takes care to point out the resemblance of Hare to Brer Rabbit and of "The Tale of Umusha Mwaice, the Little Slave Girl" to Cinderella and explains the element of cannibalism so frequently encountered in this folklore. She concludes: "My tales are meant for universal enjoyment by both adults and children; hence I have tried to keep the horror element down but not to the point where the tales lose their intrinsic African character." An example of this sort of editing is reflected in "The Hare and the Reed-buck." Instead of the innocent dupe's being killed, he is "beaten and driven from the village in disgrace."

Six of the 14 tales have as their hero Kalulu the Hare, who is a cunning, unscrupulous, mischief-loving trickster:

> The hare pretended to be dead until he thought that they had forgotten all about him. Then, gradually and silently he crept to the edge of the forest. Once out of danger he shouted, "You can't catch me or kill me either. Did you *really* think that I was dead, Foolish Ones?" And his chuckles grew fainter and fainter as he was lost to sight in the forest.

"The Lion and the Robin" resembles the fable of the saint and the mouse in the fourth book of the Hitopadesa. "Muskalalu, the Talking Skull" parallels "The Talking Skull" in Courlander's *Terrapin's Pot of Sense* (item 185). The remaining stories tell of great wonders: a lion who can change into a man, golden birds, and Akakanote, the helpful praying mantis. The stories have been "englished"; however, their varied plots make them appealing.

The well-designed volume has many lively ink drawings.

From The Fire on the Mountain, and Other Ethiopian Stories *by Harold Courlander and Wolf Leslau, illustrated by Robert W. Kane. Item 122.*

East Africa

In this area are the Sudan, Ethiopia, Uganda, Kenya, Somalia, Tanzania, and the Malagasy Republic.

Along the East Coast a particularly heavy Muslim influence is found in Swahili tales, reflecting the impact of Asian, Middle Eastern, and European folklores. Inland appear animal and trickster stories about Hare, Spider, and "Digit" (an Ethiopian Tom Thumb), stories of everyday life, and *Märchen,* many of them about ogres.

STUDIES AND COLLECTIONS FOR ADULTS

104. Beech, Mervyn W. H.
 THE SUK; THEIR LANGUAGE AND FOLKLORE. With an introduction by Sir Charles Eliot. New York, Negro Universities Press [1969]   xxiv, 151 p. illus., maps.
 GN652.S8B4 1969
Reprint of the 1911 ed.

A two-part work resulting from investigations made when the author was acting district commissioner of Baringo, East African Protectorate (later Kenya). The first part is "a sketchy and incomplete" survey of the customs of the Suk, and the second and larger part, a guide to the language. Texts of 12 animal tales and a number of riddles are rendered "as nearly as possible" in literal translation and include a variant of "The Hare and the Tortoise" ("Mr. Tortoise and Mr. Hare"). The simple tales are tersely told and lack drama. A number, such as "Sheep and Goats," "The Leopard and the Goat," "Why Some Animals Become Domestic," and "Why the Leopard Walks by Night," are how and why stories; others, such as "Rhinoceros and the Mason Bees," teach a lesson—in this case, "So you see how a little insect can get the better of a large and powerful beast."

105. Cagnolo, C.
 KIKUYU TALES. African studies, v. 11, Mar.–Sept. 1952: 1–15, 123–135; v. 12, Mar.–Sept. 1953: 10–21, 62–71, 122–131. DT751.A4, v. 11–12

Thirty tales from "a small collection" heard by the author, a missionary among the Kikuyu who "hasten[ed] to record these genuine tribal tales" before they disappeared in the name of progress and civilization. Represented here are animal stories, primarily of the trickster genre, with the Hare or Wakahare, the Squirrel, as hero and the Hyena and Lion as buffoons or dupes, and stories of everyday life. Of these, "Kemangurura, a Kikuyu Hero," repetitive in the manner of "Old Woman and the Pig," "Wamogumo and Wakagumo," with elements of "Hudden and Dudden and Donald O'Neary," "The Daughter of the Sun," in which a crippled youth wins out, "Njeri the Heroine," sacrificed to the lake that rain may fall, and "A Grateful Gazelle" could interest a reteller for children and a storyteller.

106. Dundas, *Sir* Charles.
 KILIMANJARO AND ITS PEOPLE; A HISTORY OF THE WACHAGGA, THEIR LAWS, CUSTOMS AND LEGENDS, TOGETHER WITH SOME ACCOUNT OF THE HIGHEST MOUNTAIN IN AFRICA. London, F. Cass, 1968. 349 p. illus., fold. map. (Cass library of African studies. General studies, no. 76)
 DT449.K4D8 1968

The author, who has served in British East Africa, Tanganyika Territory, Rhodesia, and the Uganda Protectorate, incorporates legends and myths in his study of the Wachagga people. Chapter 3, "Religion," deals with Ruwa, who did not create man but "liberated the first human beings from some mysterious vessel by bursting it" and is thus known as "Ruwa mopara wandu, God who burst [out] men." One of the stories remarkably akin to that of the fall of man concerns a forbidden yam: "But the yam which is called Ula or Ukaho, truly you shall not eat it . . . and if any man eats it, his bones shall break and at last he shall die." Among other motifs akin to those of the Old Testament is the theme of the coming of death (Cain and Abel). For his evil ways, man is shown to have been destroyed twice—the first time by "an immense creature," and later by flood, an occurrence common to the Old Testament, Greek mythology, and the legends of other cultures.

107. Evans-Pritchard, *Sir* Edward E.
THE ZANDE TRICKSTER. Oxford, Clarendon Press, 1967. 240 p. plates. (Oxford library of African literature)
GR360.Z28E9
Bibliography: p. 235–237.
Contents: 1. The social and cultural background.—2. Introduction to the tales.—3. The tales.—4. Some different versions.—Appendixes.

The appendixes contain two stories in Zande and English and an index to the narratives. Sources for all the tales are provided.

The texts, concerning Ture, a human trickster whose name in Zande means spider, are short and often have a Rabelaisian humor as they tell of Ture's adventures and misadventures while routinely fishing, hunting, collecting termites, and living with two wives. Often he appears as "a monster of depravity: liar, cheat, lecher, murderer; vain, greedy, treacherous, ungrateful, a poltroon, a braggart." He is completely amoral, maintaining a curious innocence in the worst of his misdeeds, often childlike, and, on occasion, revealing an unexpected kinship to Punch and Tyll Eulenspiegel. A number of his escapades are reminiscent of those of Hare, Anansi, and the American Indian Raven.

108. Gecau, Rose.
KIKUYU FOLKTALES. Nairobi, East African Literature Bureau [1970] 131 p. illus. GR360.K5G4

Eighteen tales, contained in a slim volume, have a detailed introduction in which the author surveys Kikuyu life, beliefs, and values, and analyzes the folktale as a means of instruction as well as entertainment. Dividing the tales into two large groups, those about ogres and animals (trickster tales, chiefly about Hare) and those about daily life (famine, courtship, and the like), she discusses the purpose of each genre and the techniques employed to fulfill that purpose. In conclusion she stresses the necessity of retrieving this endangered lore to "give identity to African literature . . . [and] inspiration and guidance [to creative writers] in the handling of form and expression and in developing the vitality of African verbal form in their writing."

The narratives, based on translated tape recordings, retain expressions and songs in Kikuyu. H. Owuor Anyumba in a foreword observes that this "translation at its best is fresh and strongly suggests the flavour of Kikuyu texts."

109. Hobley, Charles W.
 ETHNOLOGY OF A-KAMBA AND OTHER EAST AFRICAN TRIBES. [London] F. Cass, 1971. xvi, 172 p. illus., fold. map. (Cass library of African studies. General studies, no. 96)   DT429.H67 1971

Reprint of 1910 ed.

A concise, careful study of the cultural, social, religious, and political life of the Kamba peoples of Uganda, undertaken by a British administrator to point out "the imperative need of a training in Ethnology and Primitive Religion for those whose life task is to be the direction and control of native races in our colonies and dependencies." Chapter 21 contains seven texts: "Story of Origin of Death" (similar to the Zulu and Khoisan myth); a story of "that old favourite" in "Bantu" folklore, "The Hyaena"; "The Story of How the Animals Got Their Marks"; "The Story of the Hare, Ki-Kamba-Wa-Paruku or Buku"; "The Story of the Ngu or Tortoise and the Kipalala or Fish Eagle"; "The Cunning of the Hare"; and "Munei's Prophecy," a legend foretelling the coming of the Europeans. Trickster stories and how and why tales are also represented, each accompanied by brief comment. The story of the Tortoise and the Fish Eagle is a Hare and Tortoise story and explains the origin of the Tortoise's habit of spending part of his life in the water.

110. Hollis, *Sir* Alfred C.
 THE MASAI: THEIR LANGUAGE AND FOLKLORE. With introduction by Sir Charles Eliot. Freeport, N.Y., Books for Libraries Press, 1971. xxviii, 359 p. illus., fold. map. (The Black heritage library collection)
     PL8501.H6 1971

Reprint of the 1905 ed.

Twenty narratives, proverbs, and riddles form a section of this volume which is in part a Masai grammar and in part a description of Masai customs and traditions. The author, then chief secretary to the Administration of the East African Protectorate, has sought to record "some of the thoughts and ideas of the Masai people, before their extinction or their admixture with Bantu elements and contact with civilization renders this an impossibility." Thus, this lore, including songs and beliefs, is given in the words of the Masai themselves. An introduction by Sir Charles Eliot provides a history of the Masai people and an account of their social system.

The narratives, presented in Masai with a close linear translation followed by a literary rendition, treat most frequently such themes as the consequences of greed, cowardice, jealousy, and selfishness. A number could be adapted for storytelling, such as "The Story of the Woman and the Children of the Sycamore Tree" and "The Story of the Two Wives and the Twins". Four are retold by Verna Aardema in her *Tales for the Third Ear* (item 47).

In another section of the book, Masai Myths and Traditions, are several myths concerned with gods, the beginnings of earth, and the origin of the Masai and "Bantu" peoples. In a final section appears a legend of the medicine man Mbatian, whose story has an element of the Jacob and Esau story.

111. ———.
THE NANDI: THEIR LANGUAGE AND FOLK-LORE. With introduction by Sir Charles Eliot. Westport, Conn., Negro Universities Press [1971] 328 p. illus.   PL8545.H6 1971

Reprint of the 1909 ed.

In two parts: the first, a sociopolitical and cultural examination of the people; the second, a grammar. Nineteen narratives, a few myths, riddles, and proverbs are cited on pages 97–133. Animal stories predominate and include two stories of Hare as trickster. There are also a legend of the Nandi about a defeat of the Masai, two stories about demons who eat people, and one creation myth. A few selections would appeal to children—"The Origin of the Leopard and the Hyena"; "The Story of the Tapkōs Bird and the Child"; "The Story of the Warriors and the Devil"; "The Story of the Demon Who Ate People and the Child" (retold in item 47); "The Story of the Creation"; and "The Nandi House That Jack Built or the Old Woman and Her Pig." The last begins:

> Who will cast goats' dung at me?
> What will you do with goats' dung?
> I will throw it at the heavens.
> What do you want with the heavens?
> That they drop a little water on me.
> Why do you want a little water?
> That the burnt grass may grow. . . .

112. Knappert, Jan, *comp.*
MYTHS & LEGENDS OF THE SWAHILI. Nairobi, Heinemann

Educational Books [1970] 212 p. (African writers series, 75) GR360.S8K55

Contents: 1. Introduction.—2. The creation.—3. The prophets.—4. The miracles of Mohammed.—5. Mysterious destinies.—6. Stories of wit and wisdom.—7. The wiles of women.—8. Social satire.—9. Astute animals.—10. Travellers' tall tales.—11. Spirits and sorcerers.—12. Just judgments.

Religious and secular lore of the Swahili has been "culled from manuscripts, most of them in Arabic script, and other unpublished material written down by Swahili scholars since the early eighteenth century" and from narratives recorded by the author during the years 1961–64. He notes that variants of these stories can be found in such sources as Edward Steere's *Swahili Tales* (item 120), Carl Velten's *Märchen und Erzählungen der Suaheli* (Stuttgart, W. Spemann, 1898. xxiii, 168 p. PL8704.A2V35), and Carl Büttner's *Anthologie aus der Suaheli-Litteratur* (Berlin, E. Felber, 1894. 2 v. in 1. PL8704.B8).

In his introduction Knappert discusses the role of destiny in the lives of the people and in "the whole tapestry of Swahili mythology, secular as well as religious." He provides background for stories of the creation, accounts of the journeys of the prophets and Mohammed, and tales of the subtleties of Abu Nuwasi, the wise trickster who bears a kinship to the Turkish hodja, Nasr al-Dīn. In addition he discusses the Swahili concept of women as being "endowed with all possible vices"—a belief drummed into every boy by "almost every piece of Swahili literature."

The animal fables and travelers' tales contain many motifs encountered in the Arabian Nights stories. Other familiar elements are found in tales of spirits and stories of judges. A number of the stories could be adapted for children by the reteller and storyteller.

113. Lindblom, Gerhard.
    KAMBA FOLKLORE. Uppsala, Appelbergs boktr., 1928–35. 3 v. (Archives d'études orientales, v. 20)
    PL8351.Z77 1928
    Micro 50,812

Contents: 1. Tales of animals, with linguistic, ethnographical and comparative notes.—2. Tales of supernatural beings and adventures; texts, translations and notes.—3. Riddles, proverbs and songs; texts, translations and notes. 2. ed.

LC holds v. 2 in microform only.

The 30 animal tales in this collection are preceded by a detailed introduction in which the author, a Swedish ethnologist, discusses his method of collecting. He comments on the likelihood of inept retellings by pupils in mission or government schools and gives an example of an incomplete version. In addition he alerts the reader to a storyteller's frequent adaption of material to suit a collector's limited acquaintance with African languages.

The author divides Kamba folktales into five groups: animal tales centering around the activities of Hare, Hyena, Lion, Elephant, Tortoise, and others; *eimu* (ogre) stories; adventure stories about everyday life; myths and legends; and imported tales. He describes each genre succinctly. The texts presented in Kamba and English are rendered literally. Appended Linguistic and Ethnographic Notes and Comparative Notes add to the value of the text.

The third volume treats songs, riddles, and proverbs in a similar fashion.

114. Mbiti, John S., *ed. and tr.*
AKAMBA STORIES. Oxford, Clarendon Press, 1966. 240 p.
(Oxford library of African literature)   PL8351.M2

Bibliography: p. 41.

Part 1 describes the lifestyle of the Kamba people, their language, and literature, supplying a short bibliography and an analytical interpretation of the frequently encountered tale "The Hare, the Lion, the Hyena, and the Crow"; part 2 consists of 78 texts.

The author, a theologian and collector of roughly 1,500 narratives, who estimates that he has located 90 percent of all current Kamba stories, discusses at some length the art of storytelling, the tales themselves, and problems encountered in translation. He states that although he has "stuck closely to the Kikamba originals," he has substituted, in many instances, prose equivalents for poetry and song without, however, indicating these passages. He has provided a sampling of traditional tale openings though he has omitted the introductory phrase "The story of . . ." so often used by the Kamba. Traditional formula endings (with footnoted explanations) are employed as, for example, "You had better swing with the panther's tail while I swing with the lamb's tail" (learn to tell stories; it's better than listening).

The selection, in fluent yet compressed tellings, comprises an appealing assortment of tales dealing with warriors, chief's sons and daughters, married couples, *aimu* (ubiquitous, powerful, frequently malicious spirits), heroes with skin trouble, and animals (hares, lions, and hyenas). "The Boy Who Became King" and "The Miracle Sheep" reveal a kinship with traditional European tales. Many tales in their references to guns, lorries, white men, Asian shopkeepers, policemen, and money trees that produce "bank notes, silver shillings, and ten-cent pieces" show evidence of the impact of a modern technological society.

Stories 76 and 77 are given in Kikamba and English.

115. Millroth, Berta.
LYUBA; TRADITIONAL RELIGION OF THE SUKUMA. [Uppsala] 1965. 217 p. (Studia ethnographica Uppsaliensia, 22)
BL2480.S8M5

Akademisk avhandling—Uppsala.

Without thesis statement.

Bibliography: p. 208–214.

A documented study of the religious beliefs and customs of the Sukuma in the Lake Province of Tanganyika (Tanzania), which contains résumés of creation myths. Two detailed accounts of myths appear in chapter 5, "Myths and Traditions": The Conquest of Light and Shingwengwe or the Destruction of Man. The latter begins:

> One day a gourd (*suha* or *kisuba*) began to grow from the earth. Gradually it became uncommonly big. The children thought it very funny and said to one another: "Look, how big the gourd is." The gourd, to the consternation of everyone, said: "Look, how big the gourd is." The children said: "It speaks," and like an echo the gourd said: "It speaks." The children ran home at once and told their mothers and neighbours. Everyone hurried to see this wonderful gourd. Each in turn asked the gourd questions and the gourd repeated their questions exactly. The gourd grew and grew out of all proportion and everyone became more and more interested in it. Kings and their vassals came to see this most wonderful of gourds.
> It was then that the catastrophe happened. With a roar as of thunder the gourd burst and a monster half man and

half dragon came out of it. Its feet and its legs and arms were of fire; flames came from its eyes, and the monster ate up all the people and all the animals that were on earth.

Only one woman who was with child managed to escape destruction. . . .

116. Mushanga, Musa T., *comp.*
 FOLK TALES FROM ANKOLE. [Kampala, Uganda, Milton Obote Foundation, c1969] 144 p. illus.   GR360.B15M87

Text in English and Nyankole.

Contents: The old woman and the monster.—The coming of night.—The foolish young king.—Tinsiima.—The wise woman and her selfish husband.—The disobedient boy and his mother.—The bush that hid a man.—The man who killed his wife.—The disobedient woman and her four sons.—Kamuzinzi.—The poor, childless, kind man and his wife.—The woman who stole locusts.—The two foolish men.—The woman who gave birth to a crow.—The war between men and the monsters.—The battle of Kifunfu.—The hare and the leopard.—Hare marries leopardess.—Hare's wisdom.—A false friend.—The pig and the hyena.—The King and the hyena.

"Mr. Mushanga insists that the telling of these tales is essentially a communal activity, its purpose primarily moral; and each is followed by the precept which it is intended to convey." (Because of poor printing on thin paper, the remaining half of F. B. Welbourn's introduction, intended to explain the people's interpretations of the tales, is illegible.)

A few of the stories will interest children: "The Foolish Young King," about the wisdom of age; "Tinsiima," a variant of "Hafiz the Stone-Cutter"; "The Poor, Childless, Kind Man and His Wife," illustrating that kindness begets kindness; "The Disobedient Boy and His Mother," a "child in the drum" story; and "The Woman Who Gave Birth to a Crow," which is a "Beauty and the Beast" variant.

117. Rattray, Robert S.
 SOME FOLK-LORE STORIES AND SONGS IN CHINYANJA, with English translation and notes. With preface by Alexander Hetherwick. New York, Negro Universities Press [1969]
 224 p.   PL8593.8.R3 1969

Reprint of the 1907 ed.

Bibliographical references included in "Notes" (p. 167–224).

A three-part work intended to supplement study of the Nyanja language. In his notes the author, a government official, comments on the scarcity of "*original* native tales" and describes four commonly encountered plots: "one animal makes a laughing-stock of another, but is itself held up to ridicule"; "two animals make a covenant of friendship, each in turn doing the other some service"; "one very small animal outwits some very big one, exemplifying the proverb that wisdom is more than strength"; "people do or do not disdain to pick up some trifle, for which at the time there is no apparent use, but which after becomes of the greatest service."

Among the nine tales in this selection are "The Tortoise and the Antelope" (a variant of "The Hare and the Tortoise"); "The Story of Kachirambe" (the child born on a shin bone); two with Rabbit as trickster; and "The Blind Man and the Hunchback," which tells how the heroes rescue two daughters of a chief and become free of their infirmities.

Songs, proverbs, and riddles are interspersed.

118. Roscoe, John.
    THE BAGANDA; AN ACCOUNT OF THEIR NATIVE CUSTOMS AND BELIEFS. 2d ed. New York, Barnes & Noble [1966] xix, 547 p. illus., 3 fold. maps.   DT434.U2R7

"Bibliographical note": p. [vii]–viii.

The material in this study of the social and religious life of the Ganda was obtained first hand by the author, a missionary.

Chapter 17 deals with folklore. In a prefatory statement the author discusses the dual function of folklore in the life of the people: the first being explanatory, i.e., a means to account for "many things beyond the understanding of the people"; the second, a way of emphasizing moral truths. Thus, the people have legends of their beginnings, their kings, and gods that many accepted as "trustworthy" accounts of the origin of man and beast. The Ganda also possess a rich variety of folktales and proverbs.

The selection of 14 narratives is an attractive one, consisting of a legend of Kintu, the first man (accounting for the coming of death), a few explanatory tales, and a number with wry comment on human behavior. A section of proverbs with explanations is included.

119. Routledge, William S., *and* Katherine P. Routledge.
WITH A PREHISTORIC PEOPLE: THE AKIKUYU OF BRITISH EAST AFRICA; BEING SOME ACCOUNT OF THE METHOD OF LIFE AND MODE OF THOUGHT FOUND EXISTENT AMONGST A NATION ON ITS FIRST CONTACT WITH EUROPEAN CIVILISATION. [London] F. Cass, 1968. xxxii, 392 p. illus., facsims., fold. map, music, plans. (Cass library of African studies. General studies, no. 63)   DT429.R7 1968

Reprint of 1910 ed.

A four-part study of the Kikuyu, their pursuits, dress, arts, crafts, social and political life, and religion. Part 4 includes 13 stories—"The Maiden Who Was Sacrificed by Her Kin"; "The Lost Sister"; "The Four Young Warriors"; "A Tale Inculcating Kindness to Animals"; "The Girl and the Doves"; "The Greedy Hyena"; "The Elephants and the Hyena"; "The Giant of the Great Water"; "The Snake From the Great Water"; "M'wambia and the N'jengé"; "The Girl Who Cut the Hair of the N'jengé"; "The Forty Girls"; and "The Man Who Became a Hyena." A few legends explaining the origin of the Kikuyu people and stories of the rainbow and legendary animals are added.

The stories, originally told to children in Kikuyu, have lost dramatic fulfillment (and in "The Story of the Lost Sister" a certain logic), perhaps because of undergoing translation from Kikuyu to Swahili and thence to English. However, they have been transcribed as far as possible exactly as they were narrated, although there has been an occasional "slight alteration . . . where the language was somewhat primitive for modern taste."

A useful source for a storyteller.

120. Steere, Edward, *Bp.*
SWAHILI TALES, AS TOLD BY NATIVES OF ZANZIBAR. With an English translation. [2d ed.] London, Society for Promoting Christian Knowledge [1889] xvi, 501 p.
      PL8704.S7 1889

Twenty-one narratives, proverbs, and riddles "taken down" by the author, a missionary, as he was studying Swahili and "printed exactly as they were related." Swahili texts accompany them. Three of the narratives, "Mohammed the Languid," "The Cheat and the Porter," and "Hasseebu Kareem ed deen," originate in *The Arabian Nights*.

The tales are lengthy and represent a melange of Asian,

Middle Eastern, and Western traditional lore. "Sultan Darai" has elements of both "Cinderella" and "Puss in Boots," with a gazelle enacting the role of Puss. "Sultan Majnun" tells of the fortunes of a male Cinderella, or Ash-lad, a seventh son who succeeds, after his six brothers failed, in finding the thief who had robbed his father's date tree of its fruit. A cumulative story, "Goso, the Teacher," reminds us of "This is the House That Jack Built." The distinctiveness of the texts is enhanced by the use of such phrases as "save me from the sun, I will save you from the rain" and the formal ending "If it be good, the goodness belongs to us all, and if it be bad, the badness belongs to me who made it."

A number of these narratives are retold in *Zanzibar Tales Told by Natives of the East Coast of Africa,* translated from the original Swahili by George W. Bateman and illustrated by Walter Bobbett (GR360.Z3Z3 1969). The stories in this work, first published in 1901 and reprinted by the Afro-Am Press of Chicago, are attractively presented for young readers.

COLLECTIONS FOR CHILDREN

121. Baskerville, Rosetta G. H.
 THE KING OF THE SNAKES AND OTHER FOLK-LORE STORIES FROM UGANDA. Illustrated by Mrs. E. G. Morris. London, Sheldon Press; New York, Macmillan Co. [1922] 88 p. plates. GR360.U4B3

Uganda tales, some taken from Sir Apolo Kagwa's *Engero za Baganda,* others "picked up [by the author] . . . from old wives sitting over their cooking-pots in smoky kitchens, from porters round the camp fire at night, and from that charming mixed multitude which made up 'the good old days.'"

The compilation has variety. "The Story of Kintu" tells of the origin of death; "The Story of Mpobe" follows a hunter who wanders into the country of Death and returns. Among the animal stories is "How the Hare Traded With a Bag of Corn"; it differs from the version recorded by Torrend in *Specimens of Bantu Folk-Lore* (item 96) under the title of "My Berries" in that Hare's deceitfulness is here all but expunged from the text.

Song lyrics appear both independently and within the tales. They lack folk flavor, being translated into an English style of poetry sometimes reminiscent of Kipling.

Thirty proverbs are appended.

A second collection of tales by Mrs. Baskerville—*The Flame Tree and Other Folk-Lore Stories From Uganda*—first published in 1925, was reprinted by the Negro Universities Press in 1969.

122. Courlander, Harold, *and* Wolf Leslau.
THE FIRE ON THE MOUNTAIN, AND OTHER ETHIOPIAN STORIES. Illustrated by Robert W. Kane. New York, Holt [1950] 114 p. illus., col. plates.   GR360.E8C6

Selected and retold by collaborating folklorists, these 25 narratives represent a sampling of the diverse oral traditions of the people of Amhara, Gurage, Tigrai, Sidama, Somalia, and Eritrea. They deal with justice, the making of heroes, trickery, matchmaking, and other aspects of everyday life. One or two tales are parables; all contain wry comment on human behavior:

> Once there was a village man named Sium who had a wife who constantly made him miserable. She was quite stubborn, and always did things by opposites.
> One day when Sium wanted to build a new house he said to her, "I think we should build a round stone house."
> "No," his wife said after a moment, "we should build a square clay house."
> So the new house that Sium built was square and made of clay.
>
> From "The Contrary Woman"

In "The Ancient Land of Ethiopia" and their notes on the stories, the authors discuss cultural influences, cite Indian, African, and European equivalents, and indicate sources.

123. Davis, Russell G., *and* Brent Ashabranner, *comps.*
THE LION'S WHISKERS; TALES OF HIGH AFRICA. With illustrations by James G. Teason. Boston, Little, Brown [1959] 191 p.   GR360.E8D37

Thirty-one narratives from the Amhara, Galla, Gurage, Shankilla, Falasha, and Somali peoples of Ethiopia, gathered by the authors while on a two-year assignment assisting the Ministry of Education in the preparation of books for schools. These tales, a blend of genres, deal with justice, trickery, wisdom, and the problems of kings, often displaying ironic humor.

From Tales Told Near a Crocodile *by Humphrey Harman, illustrated by George Ford. Item 124.*

They include a story about Solomon and the Queen of Sheba, one about an Ethiopian Tom Thumb ("Digit"), a variant of "The Tortoise and the Geese," and two stories from modern everyday life—"The Long Walk" and "The Man With a Lion Head in a Can." Information about geographical areas and peoples is continuously provided in informal commentary.

124. Harman, Humphrey, *comp.*
 TALES TOLD NEAR A CROCODILE; STORIES FROM NYANZA. Illustrated by George Ford. New York, Viking Press [1967, c1962] 185 p.   GR360.K43H3 1967

From the Luo, Samia, Abaluya, Kisii, Nandi, and Masai people of Nyanza comes this collection of tales, gathered by the author while teaching in Kenya. The stories are freely translated in an informal style that enables the author to interpolate necessary background and inject occasional facetiousness. His subjects are varied—the lake (Victoria), brave men, crocodiles, cattle raids, and witch doctors. No specific sources are stated.

125. Heady, Eleanor B.
WHEN THE STONES WERE SOFT: EAST AFRICAN FIRESIDE TALES. Illustrations by Tom Feelings. New York, Funk & Wagnalls [1968] 94 p.   PZ8.1.H345 Wh

Sixteen favorite stories told to children by Mama Semamingi, "the grandmother who tells many tales." Dealing with nature, everyday life, people, and animals, they contain why stories. After providing a brief general background, the author states in her preface that she has reshaped the stories, adapting them, as did the African storytellers, for her audience. Each story with its village setting is introduced informally. African names are given to people and animals, and a few common Swahili words, like *jambo* ("hello"), are also used to convey an African flavor. Interwoven explanatory material expands the tales. In addition to not specifying her alterations, the author has not cited her sources beyond a general statement that she has drawn upon anthropological works, friends, and the staff of the Macmillan Memorial Library for materials. Tom Feelings' poetic, soft gray line-and-wash drawings underscore the mood of the stories.

From the same sources the author has compiled two collections entirely of animal stories: *Jambo, Sungura! Tales From East Africa* (illustrated by Robert Frankenberg. New York, W. W. Norton [1965] 93 p. PZ10.3.H31567 Jam) and *Safiri the Singer; East African Tales* (illustrated by Harold James. Chicago, Follett [1972] 96 p. PZ8.1.H345 Saf). Similar in presentation, the stories are told in a conversational style, which injects a fuller declaration of the characters' emotions. The character of Sungura has been modified to make him attractive. For examples of treatment of text, one may compare "Son of the Long One" (p. 60–65) and "The Ostrich Chicks" (p. 85–90) in *Jambo, Sungura!* with "The Story of the Crocodile and the Wild Animals" (p. 179–185) and "The Story of the Ostrich Chicks" in Hollis' *The Masai* (item 110). "The Scarecrow" in *Jambo, Sungura!* is a variant of the Tar Baby story.

126. Kalibala, Ernest B., *and* Mary Gould Davis.
WAKAIMA AND THE CLAY MAN, AND OTHER AFRICAN FOLKTALES. Illustrated by Avery Johnson. New York, Longmans, Green [1946] 145 p.   PZ8.1.K13 Wak

A baker's dozen of Ganda animal tales which, Mr. Kalibala notes, are "part of the education and training of children in everyday social experience." He comments further in his appended note that "each story consists of about three parts. The first part is fun. . . . The second part is the characters . . . chosen first, according to their stupidity, such as the leopard, elephant and other big animals, who, for the most part, are tricked, and second, according to their cleverness, alertness, and intelligence. . . . In the third part of the story is the moral." In his Author's Notes he provides instructions for storytellers.

The stories are appealing in their presentation—conversational with flavor furnished by songs. The selection includes a clear variant of the Tar Baby in "Wakaima and the Clay Man":

> Wanjovu had been asleep in his own bed for hours when the little figure of Wakaima stole into his potato patch. When Wakaima saw the clay man looming up in the moonlight he was frightened. Could it be Wanjovu waiting to punish him for stealing the corn and the potatoes? He dared not move. The clay man did not move. Finally Wakaima gathered courage to speak: "Hullo, Wanjovu," he called. "What are you doing here at this time of night?"
> The clay man did not answer.

127. Mesfin Habte-Mariam.
   THE RICH MAN AND THE SINGER; FOLKTALES FROM ETHIOPIA. Edited and illustrated by Christine Price. New York, Dutton [1971] 84 p. map.   GR360.E8M4 1971

Variants of many familiar tales in the European, Middle Eastern, and Asian traditions compose a large segment of this collection of stories taken primarily from the Amharic peoples by the author when a student in Addis Ababa and later a teacher in Sidamo. Among the narratives based on well-known motifs are "The Husband Who Wanted to Mind the House"; "The Meeting of the Young Mice" ("Belling the Cat"); "The Farmer and the Leopard" ("The Tiger, the Brahmin, and the Jackal"); and "Mammo the Fool" ("Epaminondas," "Clever Hans," and the like). The translations are unremarkable and lacking in flavor—no formula beginnings and endings or local expressions are employed. The tales are often didactic, although an occasional bit of satirical humor lightens the text. An introductory chapter offers a map and general information about the people and their country.

From The Rich Man and the Singer
by Mesfin Habte-Mariam, *edited and illustrated
by* Christine Price. *Item 127.*

128. Njururi, Ngumbu, *comp.*
    AGIKUYU FOLK TALES. London, Oxford University Press,
    1966. 109 p.   GR360.K5N55

The stories in this collection, dedicated "to all Kenyans living and dead who cherish and uphold our national heritage," relate to ogres, animals, and birds. Most of the narratives have interest for children, like the etiological tales "How the Wild Turkey Got Its Spots" and "The Story of the Moon and the Sun." Chants in both Kikuyu and English appear throughout the texts. Though the stories have been expanded, the basic plots appear to be unaltered.

129. Nunn, Jessie A., *comp.*
    AFRICAN FOLK TALES. Illustrated by Ernest Crichlow.
    New York, Funk & Wagnalls [1969] 141 p.   GR350.N8

Contents: Why monkeys live in trees.—Today me, tomorrow

Woodcuts by Leo and Diane Dillon from Songs and Stories from Uganda *by W. Moses Serwadda, edited by Hewitt Pantaleoni. Item 131.*

thee.—The hare and the widow.—Clowns with sad faces.—Why hawks feed on chickens.—Nyangondhu, the fisherman.—Law of the jungle.—When will animals rule the world?—The greedy wife.—Find the thief.—The miracle.—Chief Spider's problem.—Kamau, the gay bachelor.—In the old Kingdom of Kathomo.—The giant who ate people.—The black cow.—The lazy squirrel.—The sons of Murima Kwarie.—Honey and drums and a teller of tales.—The brothers.

A glossary of Swahili words and an introduction describing African storytelling preface these 20 tales from the peoples of Kenya. Descriptions of settings are woven into the story beginnings; use of Swahili words and names within the texts also convey a sense of place. Representing how and why stories, *Märchen,* and trickster tales (Hare and Spider), the narratives treat of human relationships and such traits as ingratitude, greed, and jealousy. The collection is distinctive

for its variety of plots. "The Black Cow" combines elements of "Cinderella," "Billy Beg and the Bull," and the story of Europa.

130. Osogo, John N. B.
THE BRIDE WHO WANTED A SPECIAL PRESENT, AND OTHER TALES FROM WESTERN KENYA. Kampala, East African Literature Bureau [1966] 64 p. illus.   GR360.K43O8

Contents: The beautiful bride and her hunchback sister.—The clever but lazy Nakhamuna.—The man who went to hunt.—The story of Nandagaywa.—The story of Nabutandu and his family.—The story of Nakhamuna (pt. 1).—The story of Nakhamuna (pt. 2).—The girl who ate tsinduli.—The story of Khalayi Wadolwa.—The leopard and Nakhamuna.—The bride who wanted a special present.—The story of namuluku, the shin bone.—How the people fetched fire.

The majority of stories in this collection center on the Amanani and Linani (man-eating monsters). Also here are favorite themes dealing with the child in a drum, kidnaped girls, and the ubiquitous trickster. "The Clever but Lazy Nakhamuna" is akin to the Tar Baby story.

131. Serwadda, W. Moses.
    SONGS AND STORIES FROM UGANDA. Transcribed and edited by Hewitt Pantaleoni. Illustrated by Leo and Diane Dillon. New York, Crowell [1974] 80 p.   PZ8.1.S4577 So

Includes music.

Stories translated by Serwadda from the Luganda language. The manner of their presentation is described in a prefatory note by the editor, and individual notes covering scene-setting and instructions for dancing or playing the games and chanting the songs are given for most of the 13 tales, game songs, and songs (transcribed in Western style). A guide to pronunciation is provided.

The volume is handsomely produced, with dynamic two-color woodcuts.

132. Wamugumo.
    THE TALES OF WAMUGUMO [collected] by Peter Kuguru. Illustrations by Adrienne Moore. [Nairobi] East African Pub. House [1968] 72 p. col. illus. (East African readers library no. 7)   GR360.K5W3

Eleven stories told to children by "a famous Kikuyu character" who was notorious for his enormous appetite and celebrated for his great strength and gigantic stature. In a spare, sometimes plodding style, the storyteller recounts the varied adventures of ordinary Kikuyu villagers and animals. It is interesting to note here that the Squirrel in "The Squirrel, the Leopard and the Hyena" assumes the trickster role most often assigned to Hare.

Other titles in the East African Readers Library (Nairobi, East African Pub. House) which treat of folk materials are no. 5, Charity Dahal's *The Orange Thieves*, with Beryl Moore's illustrations ([1966] 76 p. PZ4.D124Or); no. 9, J. K. Njoroge's *The Proud Ostrich, and Other Tales*, with illustrations by Adrienne Moore ([1967] 49 p. PZ7.N68Pr); and no. 10, Stephen Gichuru's *The Fly Whisk, and Other Stories From Masailand*, with Adrienne Moore's illustrations ([1967] 71 p. PZ8.1.G38 Fl).

From West Indian Folk-Tales *by Philip Sherlock, illustrated by Joan Kiddell-Monroe. Item 151.*

The West Indies

The folklore of many islands in the Antilles reflects a merging of the European and the African oral literatures with some overlay of the indigenous lore derived from Carib Indians. Chief among the islands represented in items here are Haiti, which shows the French and African worlds meeting; Jamaica and the Bahamas, representing the English and African; and Puerto Rico, with the union of the Spanish and African. Cuba, a Spanish-African area, is represented by some of the tales in *Greedy Mariani and Other Folktales of the Antilles* (item 147).

Four distinctive characters are Bouqui (evolving from the African hyena—a dupe sometimes called Uncle Bouqui) and the tricksters Malice (or Ti Malice, perhaps evolving from the African Hare), B' Rabby (or Bro Rabby—related to the African Hare), and Anansy (Spider or Spider Man—descended from the African Anansi). The oral tales have been recorded with characteristic ritual or formula beginnings and endings.

STUDIES AND COLLECTIONS FOR ADULTS

133. ANANCY STORIES AND DIALECT VERSE, by Louise Bennett [and others] With an introduction by P. M. Sherlock. Cover design after a drawing by Stella Shaw. Kingston, Jamaica, Pioneer Press [1950] 101 p.   PZ8.1.A5

These tales, proverbs, dialect verse, and songs chosen for "pleasure and delight" are introduced by Sir Philip Sherlock, who discusses the likeness of the Anansi stories to those told in West Africa (see Rattray's *Akan-Ashanti Folk-Tales*, item 40), their antiquity, and social purpose. He also comments on the proverbs, folk songs, and dialect verse.

In the stories, all but two of which are given in Jamaican dialect, Anancy either tries to "t'ief" his neighbors out of food so he won't have to work and takes revenge on them for a slight, or just stirs up enmity for the joy of it. In a Tar Baby variant, "Anancy an' Goat," Sista Nanny-goat is tricked into taking Anancy's place with the result that ". . . from dat day till teday Nanny-goat dah sey 'Bea, a Bea' an kean get noh furda. Is Anancy meck it. Jack mandoora me noh choose none." (The last six words are a traditional ending.)

A few of the tales provide a glimpse into social changes, as in "Anancy and Ticks":

> Once upon a time Anancy an Ticks use fe live next door to one anada. Anancy had a goat an Ticks had a cow, but Anancy coulda read and Ticks could'n read. An eena dem deh days we nevah got noh Literacy campaign. . . .

134. Beckwith, Martha W.
JAMAICA ANANSI STORIES; with music recorded in the field by Helen Roberts. New York, American Folk-Lore Society, 1924. 295 p. (Memoirs of the American Folk-Lore Society, v. 17)   GR1.A5, v. 17

The author states in her preface that the stories were taken from over 60 Negro storytellers in "remote country districts" in 1919 and 1921. Here are Animal Stories, Old Stories, Chiefly of Sorcery, Modern European Stories, Song and Dance, and a few pages of Witticisms and Riddles. The folklorist notes that they are "set down without polish or adornment, as nearly as possible as they were told to me, and hence represent, so far as they go, a true folk art." Songs and music mingle with texts. All of it—the storytelling, riddling, and song—is called "Anansi story." In Jamaica, where these stories and riddles played so important a part in the lives of the people, "Two influences have dominated story-telling . . . the first an absorbing interest in the magical effect of song which, at least in the old witch tales, far surpasses that in the action of the story; the second, the conception of the spider Anansi as the trickster hero among a group of animal figures." The folklorist points to the Jamaican Anansi's kinship to Anansi, Turtle, and Hare of Africa and to the American Brer Rabbit.

Among elements parallel to those in African tales are playing godfather, the trickster and glutton in the cow's belly, the false bride, the warning bird, the riding horse, and the Tar Baby:

> Tiger got a groun' plant some peas an' get Hanansi to

watch it. Me'while Hanansi are de watchman, himself stealin' de peas. Tiger tar a 'tump, put on broad hat on de 'tump. Hanansi come.

Among the European tales is a Jack and the Bean-stalk:

Jack's father died an' leave he an' his mother. And all them money finish an' they didn't have more than one cow leave. An' the mother gave him to go to the market an' sell it. When he catch part of the way, he swap it for a cap of bean.

"Big Claus and Little Claus" appears as "Big Begum and Little Begum," and a Hansel and Gretel story as "The Children and the Witch."

Includes Index to Riddles, Abbreviations of Titles (bibliography: p. [223]–232), Notes to the Tales, and Index to Informants.

135. Comhaire-Sylvain, Suzanne.
CREOLE TALES FROM HAITI. Journal of American folk-lore, v. 50, July/Sept. 1937: 207–295; v. 51, July/Sept. 1938: 219–346.   GR1.J8, v. 50–51

Bibliography: p. [xxvii]–lxiii.

"Tales With Human Characters" (with and without supernatural elements); "Tales of Men and Supernatural Beings"; and "Tales of Animal or Devil Spouses" are presented in Creole and in English. Both the texts and their footnotes, which supply explanatory data, names of informants, and parallels, make a rich source for the reteller and scholar.

A detailed description of the richness of Haitian folklore—its folktales, their structure, form, style, language, use of song, presentation, and diffusion—is provided by the author in her thesis, *Les Contes haitians* (Paris, 1937. 2 v. GR121.H3C6). In this work a number of tales are fully analyzed as to parallels, variants, themes, motifs, and origins.

The author has also produced *Le Roman de Bouqui* (Port-au-Prince, Haiti [Impr. du Collège Vertières] 1940. 116 p. PQ3949.C63R6), a collection of 25 tales about Bouqui and Malice, together with discussion of their African origin and relationship to such African characters as Hare.

136. Courlander, Harold.
THE DRUM AND THE HOE; LIFE AND LORE OF THE HAITIAN PEOPLE. Berkeley, University of California Press, 1960.

xv, 371 p. illus.   GR121.H3C65 1960

"The music: musical notations by Mieczyslaw Kolinski of 186 songs and drum rhythms": p. [203]–313.

"Bibliography and discography": p. [363]–366.

A work designed "to present a broad view of certain aspects of Haitian culture and wherever possible to extract some of the flavor of Haitian thinking as well as its sense." In his prefatory remarks the folklorist comments on variations in Haitian mores and beliefs, the importance of Vodoun (religious practices rooted in West Africa) in the lives of many of the people, and the recording of the songs and stories.

Between the chapters describing life and customs of the people and their music, song, and dance, is chapter 16, devoted to "Folk tales: Bouqui, Malice, and Jean Saute." Courlander talks of the powerful assimilation in Haiti of stories from many cultures—European, African, Middle Eastern, Asian, and American, both North and Latin; the close ties of West Africa's Hare and Spider to Brer Rabbit in the United States, the Hare of Thailand, and the Mouse Deer of Indonesia; and the seemingly endless Haitian repertoire. He sees Haitian adaptations or simplifications of European stories of kings, princesses, and Stupid John or Jean Saute and Smart John or Jean L'Esprit, as well as Haitian changes in such African tales as "Anansi's Tug of War." Anansi, he writes, survives in Jamaica as Brother Anansi, Sister Nancy, and Nancy, and in Haiti and other islands of the Antilles chiefly as Ti Malice and Nonc' Bouqui, two men who share Anansi's characteristics. Ti Malice inherits the wiliness and wit, Bouqui the stubbornness, gluttony, and stupidity. Samples of typical tales are provided.

Appendixes deal with Haitian gods, or *loa,* from both Dahomey and the Congo, and with games and proverbs. They provide notes on orthography, translations of songs, and a glossary of Creole terms used in the text. Additional details about the stories are supplied in the Notes (p. [349]–355).

137. Crowley, Daniel J.
 I COULD TALK OLD-STORY GOOD: CREATIVITY IN BAHAMIAN FOLKLORE. Berkeley, University of California Press, 1966. 156 p. map. (University of California publications. Folklore studies, 17)   GR40.C73

An analysis of the role of the narrator in Bahamian oral tradition. The author speaks of the research of Charles L.

Edwards and Elsie Clews Parsons, as well as of his own method of collecting tales and approach to this study. He considers the people and their lifestyles and the tales (how, when, and why they are told and to whom), spirituals, sermons, proverbs, and narratives which are not considered "old-stories" by the Bahamians. These latter deal with spirits, Chickchannies (magic birds), Yehos (spirits), Little Red Men, and the dead. Further, he discusses the style and structure of the old-stories, their inclusion of song, and formulas for opening and closing.

The texts "have been transcribed in standard English spelling, but without altering word order or any other feature of Bahamian speech." Some dialect spelling has been used and colloquialisms and profanity retained.

Forty-two Booky-Rabby tales, a cycle of trickster tales, and a melange of 42 non-Booky-Rabby tales are presented, with their narrators and techniques described in detail. Many of the stories are seen to have African origins. In respect to their existence in the various islands, Crowley comments on regional differences, individual narrators and their differences, their creativity, the narrators' evaluation of the tales, and the relationship of folktale to theater. He concludes: "As the kaleidoscope produces a new and unique design at each shaking, so the Bahamian folktale is a new and unique story at each retelling."

A scholarly work intended for the serious student, with an appendix "Comparative Materials," a bibliography, and an index to tales.

138. Des Prés, François Marcel-Turenne.
    CHILDREN OF YAYOUTE; FOLK TALES OF HAITI. Port-au-Prince, Haiti, H. Deschamps, 1949. 180 p.
    GR121.H3D4 1949

Tales of Bouqui and Malice, "based on original stories handed down through many generations and . . . told by the peasants" in the Haitian mountains. The author remarks that though there are those who believe that the two related characters (uncle and nephew) were animals, "others hold that they were Africans who came among the earliest slaves and remained in Haiti until they died. But because of the many stories and jokes told about them, their names still live among the Haitian peasants." He then describes the two, so often encountered as uncle and nephew—the shrewdness of Malice, who some say "was not an African of pure blood," and the alertness or cunning which led him to be associated with the African Hare; and the stupidity and clumsiness of his

dupe, the "confused, thick-tongued, greedy" Bouqui.
Here is the traditional beginning:

> —Cric?
> —Crac! —would reply the audience, jumping up wide awake.
> —Time-time?—(Pronounce Team-team) . . .
> —Dry wood!—the audience would reply, meaning that they wanted to hear stories.
> —How many branches? . . .
> —Thirty-three branches!—the audience might answer indicating the number of stories they wanted to be told that evening.

The stories are flavorful, containing enough local expressions and phrases to give them zest. Familiar motifs include the trickster inside the cow's belly, selling mothers, and playing godfather:

> —Cric?
> —Crac!
>
> Malice knew that Bouqui had a calabash of honey hidden in his house which he had been saving for Independence Day. For sometime he had been scheming to get to it. He loved honey, even four times more than Bouqui. But he could never get Bouqui out of the house long enough to look for the calabash.
>
> After days of planning, he decided to invite Bouqui to help him weed his field of corn. . . .
> . . . Malice jumped to his feet. "Listen."
> "What?"
> "Didn't you hear somebody calling me?"
>
> From "How Malice Drunk the Honey"

139. Edwards, Charles L.
BAHAMA SONGS AND STORIES. A CONTRIBUTION TO FOLKLORE. Boston, Published for the American Folk-Lore Society, by Houghton, Mifflin, 1895. 111 p. illus., plates. (Memoirs of the American Folk-Lore Society, v. 3)
GR121.B3E3

Songs and stories in the Bahamian dialect illustrate the "genetic relation existing between the tales and music of the Bahamas and of the United States negro. . . . Parallels from accessible collections of American, and of native African, folk-lore are indicated." These were collected in 1888 at Green

Turtle Cay; in 1891, at Harbour Island; and, in 1893, at Bimini. Some of the stories and part of the introduction appeared first in the *American Journal of Psychology*, v. 2, 1889, and in the *Journal of American Folk-Lore*, v. 4, 1891.

In his introduction the biologist-author describes the islands, their composition, industries, and inhabitants, and pays particular attention to the "colored" people from whom the songs and stories were gathered. He notes that the stories fall into two classifications—"old stories," i.e., black folklore, and fairy stories, some of which have been "translated" into "old stories." Here folklore proper consists primarily of animal stories, often about the adventures of B'Rabby, a cousin of Brer Rabbit. They reveal familiar types and are "most popular" with children who tell or "talk" old stories in the early evening.

In "B'Helephant and B'Vw'ale," there is a variant of the tug of war story; in "B'Loggerhead and B'Conch," "The Hare and the Tortoise," and in "B'Rabby an' B'Tar-Baby," the Tar Baby. "B'Hellibaby and B'Dawndejane," with the cave, the password of "Open she-she, open!", and the jug episode, shows a relationship to "Ali Baba and the Forty Thieves."

Märchen or retold variants of European tales have been shortened considerably over the years and are often garbled. "B' Little-Clod an' B' Big-Clod," the Bahamian form of "Big Claus and Little Claus" or "Great Claus and Little Claus," begins:

> Once it vwas a time, a very good time,
> De monkey chewed tobacco, an' 'e spit white lime.
> B'Little-Clod had one horse and B'Big-Clod had two. B'Big-Clod use to take B'Little-Clod's hoss an' to work 'im, and use to give 'im nothin' to heat. B'Little-Clod get wexed. An' 'e vwent to take B'Big-Clod's hoss to work too. Vwen 'e vwent to take 'is hoss, B'Big-Clod slapped B'Little-Clod down an' 'e sent 'im avay. 'E say, "Jus' le' me sleep here to-night!" 'E sleep alongside 'is granfader, B'Little-Clod. B'Big-Clod put B'Little-Clod in front, an' put 'is granfader over back. An' B'Little-Clod 'e vwent over back, an' put 'is granfader in front. An' B'Big-Clod come an' 'e cut off 'is granfader's head because 'e t'ought it vwas B'Little-Clod. . . . "

"Greo-Grass an' Hop-o'-my-Thumb" combines elements of "Jack the Giant-Killer" and Charles Perrault's "Hop o' my Thumb": "Hop-o'-my-Thumb had five brudders, an' hevery one on 'em vwas bigger 'n him; 'e vwas de younges', an' 'e vwas only as big as you' little thumb."

A work of interest to the researcher, reteller, and student of folklore.

140. Iremonger, Lucille.
    WEST INDIAN FOLK-TALES: ANANSI STORIES, TALES FROM WEST INDIAN FOLK-LORE, retold for English children. Illustrated by Michael Ross. London, G. G. Harrap [1956] 64 p.   GR120.I7

Ten of the "best-known and most loved of . . . [the Anansi] stories" have been "translated" by the author from the dialect in which she first heard them as a child from her nana. She adds further that when necessary, she removed from the texts "layers of Grimm's Fairy Tales and Walt Disney until their true form was laid bare."

Motifs encountered in African Jamaican stories come together in different combinations. "How Spider People Came To Live in Webs" begins with Anansi stealing crops from Brer Monkey and Brer Tiger, who find him out. Anansi hides in a little grain of corn; the corn is swallowed whole by a hen:

> So Brer Anansi was in the corn, and the corn was in the hen.
> A little later the hen went down to a pool to drink.
> There was an alligator in the pool, and the alligator rose to the surface and saw the hen and snapped her up. Down his throat she went, and so Brer Anansi was in the corn, and the corn was in the hen, and the hen was in the alligator, and the alligator was in the pool.

Brer Tiger and Brer Monkey learn of his whereabouts from their magic drum; they locate the alligator, cut him open, find the hen and then the corn. Anansi runs. He saves his life by spinning a web: "And that is how Anansi the spider-god came to live in a web and learned to eat butterflies for his dinner."

> Jack Mandory,
> The story is ended.

Adding to the appeal of the stories is the repetition of significant phrases, such as Brer Tiger's "And after that I am going to kill you!" in "How Brer Tiger Came To Walk on Four Legs," a variant of the favorite riding horse story.

141. Jekyll, Walter, *ed.*
    JAMAICAN SONG AND STORY; ANNANCY STORIES, DIGGING SINGS, RING TUNES, AND DANCING TUNES. With new intro-

ductory essays by Philip Sherlock, Louise Bennett and Rex Nettleford. New York, Dover Publications [1966] xv, 288 p.   GR121.J2J4 1966

Includes unacc. melodies.

"An unabridged and unaltered republication of the work first published . . . in 1907."

Three new essays include first Sir Philip Sherlock's account of Jamaican life and history. Following, Louise Bennett shares her childhood memories of hearing and telling the Annancy stories. She states: "At the end of each story, we had to say, 'Jack Mandora, me no chose none,' because Annancy sometimes did very wicked things in his stories, and we had to let Jack Mandora, the doorman at heaven's door, know that we were not in favor of Annancy's wicked ways. 'Me no chose none' means 'I don't choose to behave in any of these ways.'" Rex Nettleford notes the importance of the Annancy songs and stories in the theater.

Alice Werner, in the introduction included here from the original edition, discusses ties between the Jamaican Annancy and African Anansi stories, possible origins, and relationships to the African Tortoise and Hare and the American Brer Rabbit.

In a preliminary statement Jekyll describes Annancy (his trickery, laziness, selfishness, and manner of speech—he has a cleft palate and speaks through his nose), the language of the tales and its pronunciation, and the tunes. The stories are short and vigorous in their telling, many contain songs or tunes, and each is followed by an explanatory note. Among the varied tales is one explaining why Annancy lives in the housetop and another telling how Annancy guesses the names of the King's daughters, marries the youngest "an' a reign./ Annancy is the wickedest King ever reign. Sometime him / dere, sometime him gone run 'pon him rope and tief cow fe him wife. / *Jack Mantora me no choose none.*" Occasionally Annancy gets a deserved comeuppance, as in "How Monkey Manage Annancy" and "Man-Crow."

142. Johnson, Gyneth.
    HOW THE DONKEYS CAME TO HAITI, AND OTHER TALES. Illustrated by Angelo di Benedetto. New York, Devin-Adair Co., 1949. 86 p.   PZ8.1.J6 Ho

Stories collected in the early 1940's when the author and her husband were living in Haiti in a "native *caille* among the country people." In an "Author's Note" she summarizes Haitian history, describes the people, their way of life, and language (a patois), and discusses their presentation of stories in "Sings," which were "almost always held during the full of the moon." Here also she indicates favorite themes and comments on the effect of Spanish and French cultures on the "native" African heritage to produce the "exotic blend essentially Haitian."

Among the stories two types are found throughout the African oral tradition: tales of girls who marry demons in disguise ("The Girl Who Married a Stranger" and "Demon Loango") or men who wed beasts disguised as beautiful women, and people swallowed whole by demons ("The Coming of Day and Night").

143. Parsons, Elsie W. C., *ed.*
FOLK-TALES OF ANDROS ISLAND, BAHAMAS. Lancaster, Pa., American Folk-Lore Society, 1918. xx, 170 p. music. (Memoirs of the American Folk-Lore Society, v. 13)
GR121.B3P3

Bibliography: p. xvii–xx.

In her introduction the author describes Andros, its population, history, and "ol' storee" with patterned openings and closings, stock characters—the crafty Rabbit, the greedy, slow-moving Bouqui, the hero Jack or Jock, and the heroine Greenleaf—and "sings." The tales, each with bibliographic notes, have been grouped "historically" and, on occasion, by provenience.

Among familiar elements are the feigning of death, the Tar Baby, the good child and the bad, the riding horse, the demon/devil/witch spouse, the tug of war (Rabby tricking Elephin and W'ale into pulling against each other), the fake funeral, and the guessing of a name.

Many of the tales have counterparts in other cultures—African, European, and the United States. "The Password: In the Cow's Belly" is found in West Africa, southern Africa, the West Indies, Georgia, Louisiana, and elsewhere. "Playing Godfather" is encountered in Louisiana and Georgia, in Africa, and in Europe (The Grimms' "The Cat and The Mouse Set Up Housekeeping"). It begins:

> Once was a time, a very good time,
> Monkey chew tobacco an' spit white lime.
> Once Boukee an' Rabby went on de bay an' pick up a kag of butter, an' dey car'ed de butter home. An' b'o'

Rabby say, "Now, b'o' Boukee, we cut fiel' togeder." Say, "You'll he'p me to-day, an' I'll he'p you to-morrow." So dey went to start ter cut de fiel'. Directly b'o' Rabbit holler out, "Say!" Boukee say, "Rabby, who call you?"—"Dem people might call me. Dey can't name chillun dey se'f. I ain't goin' noway." B'o' Boukee say, "Go 'long, 'cause only you here could name chillun." Say, "All right, I goin' dis time; but if dey call again, I ain't goin' no more." He went an' he opened de kag of butter, an' he started to eat. An' when he went back, b'o' Boukee ax him, "What de chil' name?" Say, "I gi' him name 'Begin um.'"

Stories like "Jack Bean" are considerably shorter than their European counterparts:

His fader died an' lef' a cow. Dey had dis cow. De mother was compelled to sell it by bein' poorer. So one day more than all, a man come by, an' asked de moder if she would like to sell de cow. So she says, "Yes." So she asked him what would he give her for de cow. He said, "I will give you a bean. . . . Dis bean will be the instigation of you havin' a fortune if you have a boy."

A source for research and possible retellings.

144. Parsons, Elsie W. C.
FOLK-LORE OF THE ANTILLES, FRENCH AND ENGLISH. New York, American Folk-Lore Society, G. E. Stechert, 1933. 2 v. (Memoirs of the American Folk-Lore Society, v. 26)
GR1.A5, v. 26

Tales, riddles, proverbs, and verses collected by the author during 1924, 1925, and 1927 on visits to the many islands of the Antilles. She speaks of her local assistants, her recording of the material, and the richness of folklore in the former French islands in contrast to that of the Dutch, former Danish, and northerly British islands. In conclusion she indicates the importance of the islands, particularly those which are French-speaking, to the student of the relationship of African culture to that of the black in America. The stories, numbered under each island (for example, 95 for Martinique), are arranged geographically from south to north; they appear usually in French creole, with a number also in English, their variants included.

Among characters encountered in the stories are Ti-Malice, Bouqui, Rabbit, Bu or Bo Nancy, Jean Sotte, Jean L'Espwit

(Stupid John and Clever John) and 'Tit Jean. Some have the formula beginning: "Cric! Crac!" Some are adaptations of European tales, such as "La Belle et la bête" or "Beauty and the Beast." Others show a relationship to Africa, like "In the Cow's Belly" and "Rabbit Went To Ask God for a Little Bit of Wisdom." Many of the story patterns are well known. Tar Baby elements appear in "Wax Doll (Take My Place!): Tiger Listens to World Below: Rabbit Spat on Me!" (No. 7 in the Trinidad stories):

> Water hole, Rabbit mess up water, could not get water. Dey make wax doll, teacup of chocolate in one hand, bread in other. Rabbit ask chocolate. Doll don't answer. Rabbit say, "Goin' to lash you . . ." Rabbit stick. People came, held him.

In another variant told in Trinidad, the place of Rabbit is taken by Compé' Saiyen (Spider). "Tar Baby: Eavesdropper: Without Scratching," as told in Anguilla centers on Nancy, "a wery wise man" who steals yams from "Father Gad."

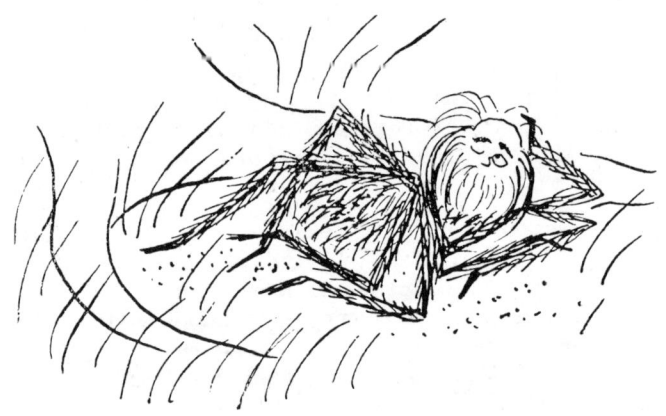

From Anansi, the Spider Man; Jamaican Folk Tales *by Philip Sherlock, illustrated by Marcia Brown. Item 149.*

COLLECTIONS FOR CHILDREN

145. Alegría, Ricardo E.
THE THREE WISHES; A COLLECTION OF PUERTO RICAN FOLKTALES. Translated by Elizabeth Culbert. Illustrated by Lorenzo Homar. New York, Harcourt, Brace & World [1969] 128 p. PZ8.1.A355 Th

Hispanic, "aboriginal," and African influences are reflected in this collection of Puerto Rican folktales which has been "slightly adapted for children." "Some of these traditional stories," the author notes, "originated in the Orient and were carried to Spain by the Arabs. . . . Others were brought from West Africa by the Negro slaves. After countless retellings they have been adapted to the geography and cultural environment."

Among the tales with motifs common in Africa are "The Rabbit and the Tiger," which begins with Rabbit pretending to be dead in order to steal Tiger's cheeses, and "The Singing Sack," about a young girl who left her golden earrings by the river and was captured by an old man who thrust her into a sack and made her sing:

> Your golden earrings, Mother,
> I tried to keep dry.
> So in this sack I smother,
> For earrings I must die.

146. Belpré, Pura.
THE TIGER AND THE RABBIT, AND OTHER TALES. Illustrated by Tomie de Paola. Philadelphia, Lippincott Co. [1965] 127 p. PZ8.1.B4127 Ti 2

A selection of stories heard by the author when he was a child "growing up on the island of Puerto Rico in an atmosphere of natural story-tellers." Augusta Baker, former coordinator of Children's Services in the New York Public Library, remarks in her foreword that these particular stories were first told by the author in library story hours, where the children were quick to recognize likenesses of the Puerto Rican "The Dance of the Animals," to the African "How Mr. Elephant Got a New Hind End" and of the Puerto Rican "The Albohaca Plant" to the Czechoslovakian "Clever Manka." Most of the stories reflect the Hispanic culture; however, "The Tiger and the Rabbit" and "The Wolf, the Fox, and the Jug of Honey" bear a relationship to stories told in Africa.

This volume adds three Hispanic stories to the original edition (Boston, Houghton Mifflin, 1946, illustrated by Kay Peterson Parker): "The Cat, the Mountain Goat, and the Fox," "The Three Petitions," and "The Three Figs," while a different "Juan Bobo" has been substituted for that in the earlier book.

147. Carter, Dorothy S., *comp.*
GREEDY MARIANI AND OTHER FOLKTALES OF THE ANTILLES. Illustrated by Trina Schart Hyman. New York, Atheneum, 1974. 131 p.   PZ8.1.C2277 Gr

"A Margaret K. McElderry book."

From Greedy Mariani and Other Folktales of the Antilles *by Dorothy S. Carter, illustrated by Trina Schart Hyman. Item 147.*

Tales of How and Why, Animal Tales, Annancy Tales, A Ti Malice Tale, Tales of Magic, and Tales of People—from Cuba, Puerto Rico, Haiti, Jamaica, the Dominican Republic, and other islands in the Antilles—have been adapted for children from French, Spanish, and English printed sources. Among the characters encountered here are Puerto Rico's Juan Bobo and Compae Rabbit, Montserrat's Brer Rabbit, and Jamaica's Annancy. The flavor of the originals has been preserved by the inclusion of songs and such phrases as *"Pues, ten cuidado! . . .* (A forceful way of saying, 'Watch out!')."

Explanatory details are worked into the text skillfully without excessive elaboration. "Why Misery Remains in the World" bears a relationship to "Wicked John and the Devil," for Aunt Misery catches Death in her pear tree in the same way that John caught the Devil in his firebush. "The Miser Who Received His Due" tells of a slave who outwitted a cruel master:

> There once was a miser so miserly that for a few silver coins he was capable of tossing his soul to the Devil. . . .
> With his slaves this miser enjoyed a reputation for cruelty and injustice. . . .
> One of the slaves, Tito, the most badly treated and amply flogged of the lot, had still enough spirit to wish to repay the master for his bounty of whippings.
> "I will make a wager," he told his companion slaves one evening, "that by the use of my wits I will, before a month is out, be seated at my master's table."

148. Courlander, Harold.
 THE PIECE OF FIRE, AND OTHER HAITIAN TALES. Illustrated by Beth and Joe Krush. New York, Harcourt, Brace & World [1964] 128 p. GR121.H3C66 1964

Animal, trickster, *enfant terrible,* and Bouqui-Malice stories are among the genres in this rich collection. Lacking only are the *cante fables* and demon stories. In "Some Comments on Haitian Folk Tales" the folklorist-author discusses the relationship of Bouki and Ti Malice to West Africa's Anansi the Spider, "a curious combination of trickster and buffoon, celebrated for his cleverness but sometimes victimized by his own stupidity." He pays attention to the intermeshing of European and African traditions with the Haitian, the telling of the stories, and formula endings and beginnings:

> "Ladies and gentlemen, good evening. Tonight we shall have a story. It will not be a story that is too long. It will not be a story that is too short!"

These are not employed in the texts, the folklorist notes, as they would appear distracting in print. Background information, comments on variants, sources, and themes are supplied in Notes on the Stories.

A number of the tales have appeared in the author's now out of print *Uncle Bouqui of Haiti* (New York, W. Morrow, 1942. 129 p. illus. PZ8.1.C8 Un) and *The Drum and the Hoe; Life and Lore of the Haitian People* (item 136).

Collections for Children   119

From Uncle Bouqui of Haiti *by Harold Courlander, illustrated by Lucy Herndon Crockett. See item 148.*

Beth and Joe Krush's line-drawings carry out the humor of these tellable, appealing narratives.

149. Sherlock, *Sir* Philip M.
     ANANSI, THE SPIDER MAN; JAMAICAN FOLK TALES. Illustrated by Marcia Brown. New York, Crowell [1954]
     112 p.   PZ8.1.S54 An

The 14 stories, retold for children by a well-known Jamaican educator, reveal close ties with those about Anansi of West Africa. In this account Anansi wins the ownership of the stories from Tiger in much the same manner as his West African cousin wins them from the Sky-god (see Rattray's story "How It Came About that the Sky-God's Stories Came To Be Known as Spider Stories" in *Akan-Ashanti Folk-Tales,* item 40). In other tales Anansi practices successful skullduggery to get food: in "Anansi in Fish Country" he pretends to be a fish doctor and eats his patient; in "Anansi and the Plantains" he tricks Rat into giving him food for his family

and then connives to have the family give most of it to him.
Marcia Brown's spirited line drawings equal the tales in humor.

150. ———.
THE IGUANA'S TAIL; CRICK CRACK STORIES FROM THE
CARIBBEAN. Illustrated by Gioia Fiammenghi. New York,
Crowell [1969] 97 p.   PZ8.1.S54 Ig

In a preface addressed to children, the author defines the Crick Crack story as any tale beginning with the traditional beginning of

> Crick crack
> Break my back.

The six animal stories in this collection are in a narrative frame with a forest setting, where the animals take turns telling stories at night while they rest from their long journey in quest of food and water. They tell of Frigate Bird and how he lost his beak to Pelican; of Old Woman Crim (the witch) and her friend Dry Bone, the "old skin-and-bone" man; of a race between Donkey and Toad, Tortoise who learned to fly, and other creatures. Some of the stories bear a kinship to tales found in Africa.

151. ———.
WEST INDIAN FOLK-TALES. Illustrated by Joan Kiddell-Monroe. New York, H. Z. Walck, 1966. 151 p. illus. (part col.) (Myths and legends series)   GR120.S5 1966

In his introduction the author writes of the Carib and Arawak Indians, their destruction by Europeans, and the coming of the African with his "memories of ancient people and far-away lands, of Ashanti-land, and Dahomey, Congoland and Iboland, of the Yorubas, the Fanti, and the Mandingo people." Among survivals of this African heritage are songs sung in Haiti about Africa and stories of Anansi the spider heard in Jamaica, Barbados, Antigua, Trinidad, Grenada, and Guiana. Sir Philip describes Anansi as sometimes human—"A little bald-headed man with a falsetto voice" and a limp and a lisp, who lives by his wits—and comments briefly on the stories.

Most of the tales are centered about Anansi. Two of them, "Tiger Story, Anansi Story" and "Work-Let-Me-See," are based on "From Tiger to Anansi" and "Brother Breeze and the Pear Tree" in Sherlock's earlier *Anansi, the Spider Man* (item 149). They tell of Anansi's attempts to get food without working by outwitting Snake, Rabbit, and Tiger (the last being not a true tiger, the author suggests, but perhaps a leopard). Other stories deal with such connivings as Anansi's unsuccessful attempt to steal the king's daughter from the brave young man who had won her.

Motifs common to African folklore are evident. Attractive black-and-white drawings and a few with color added break the text pleasingly.

The United States

The African tale entered the United States in lore dominated by the animal story. Here the African trickster—Spider, Tortoise, or Hare—merges in the more gentle, but no less cunning, Brer Rabbit or Buh Rabbit. Joel Chandler Harris initiated the recording of stories in a form that was more literary than folk. Others followed him, setting down nostalgic recollections of stories heard in their plantation childhoods permeated by the white re-creation of the myth of the happy pre-Civil War South, showing an almost idyllic relationship between master and slave and the childlike black happily existing in a protected world.

This wave of collecting was continued by folklorists and other interested persons whose recorded tales appeared in folklore journals, such as the *Journal of American Folklore* and *Southern Folklore Quarterly* (v. 1+ Mar. 1937+ Jacksonville, Fla., H. & W. B. Drew Co., GR1.S65). Recording of folktales was also done under the Work Projects Administration. All were set down exactly as heard, without extension or elaboration of texts.

In addition to animal tales there are fragments and some stories revealing the black's passionate yearning to be free, such as the legend of flying Africans (see item 153). There are also tales of human tricksters, like the slave John who outwits Old Massa. And there is the evolution of the "bad guy" hero —a gentler version of this figure would be Daddy Mention, whose specialty was escaping from prison—and folk heroes like Stagalee, with his completely amoral character, and Railroad Bill, who was "bad" but nevertheless helped his own people. Most famous of the black folktale characters was John Henry, the "steel-driving man."

Illustration by *A. B. Frost* from
The Complete Tales of Uncle Remus
by Joel Chandler Harris. Item *162*.

STUDIES AND COLLECTIONS FOR ADULTS

152. Bacon, A. M., *and* Elsie W. C. Parsons.
FOLK-LORE FROM ELIZABETH CITY COUNTY, VIRGINIA.
Journal of American folk-lore, v. 35, July/Sept. 1922: 250–327.   GR1.A533, v. 35

A collection of tales and riddles gathered by Miss Bacon "two decades or more ago" when she "conducted a folk-lore society in Hampton Institute." Animal, witch, and noodle-head are among the story types.

Elsie Clews Parsons, as editor, comments briefly in her preface on the noodle-head story and on her own work in Virginia.

"Pamelance," one of the noodle-heads, begins:

> 'Bout a boy named Pamelance. His mother sent him to his aunty's, an' she gave him some butter; an' he put the butter up in his hat, an' it melted all down over his face. And when he got home, his mother said, "Lord-dee mussy, Pamelance! What dat you got dere, boy?" He said, "Butter, mammy."—"Don'tcher know dat's not de way to carry butter? You ought to take it and put it in a leaf, and take it to the water an' cool it an' cool it an' cool it." So the next day he went to his aunty's she gave him a little puppy; and he took it to the water and cooled it and cooled it and cooled it 'til it died; an' then he brought it home. His mother said, "Lord-dee mussys, Pamelance . . . !"

In this parallel to the famous Epaminondas story, only the incident of the pies is missing.

153. Botkin, Benjamin A., *ed.*
A TREASURY OF SOUTHERN FOLKLORE; STORIES, BALLADS, TRADITIONS, AND FOLKWAYS OF THE PEOPLE OF THE SOUTH. With a foreword by Douglas Southall Freeman. New York, Crown Publishers [1949] xxiv, 776 p. music.
GR108.B6

An ample compendium of southern traditions, customs, and tales. The editor-compiler describes the Southland—its inhabitants, diverse folkways, and culture. Selections from black Americans appear in "Fables and Myths." These tales include "Flying Africans," earlier found under the title "All God's Chillen Had Wings" in *The Doctor to the Dead; Grotesque*

Legends and Folk Tales of Old Charleston, by John Bennett (Westport, Conn., Negro Universities Press [1973, c1946] 260 p. illus. GR103.B4 1973). Botkin's version begins:

> Once all Africans could fly like birds; but owing to their many transgressions, their wings were taken away. There remained, here and there in the sea islands and out-of-the-way places in the low country, some who had been overlooked, and had retained the power of flight, though they looked like other men.
> There was a cruel master on one of the sea islands.

154. Bowman, James C.
JOHN HENRY, THE RAMBLING BLACK ULYSSES. Illustrated by Roy La Grone. Chicago, A. Whitman, 1942. 288 p. plates (part col.) PS461.J6B6

Includes songs with music.

Taking scraps of ballads, songs, folk beliefs, and other fragments from oral tradition, the author of *Pecos Bill* has given, in literary form, his interpretation of the John Henry legend. Here is John Henry, a "wonder child," a devoted slave freed after his master's death, who became "a powerful steel-drivin' man" and "beat de steamer drill down, An' he died wid his hammer in his hand."

155. Bradford, Roark.
JOHN HENRY. Woodcuts by J. J. Lankes. New York, Harper, 1931. 225 p. col. plate. PS3503.R2215J6 1931

A reworking of the John Henry legend in which John Henry, a laborer of prodigious size and strength, encounters Stacker Lee, is pursued by women, loves and is often deserted by his Julie Ann, and ends up rolling cotton against a steam winch:

> Then lightning cleaved the air and the sky turned black like night. The Mississippi River ran uphill and the earth shook like a feather. The sun blazed out like a ball of fire, and started to set across the river. And when John Henry saw the sun was about to go down, he reached out with his long cotton hook and stuck it nine inches deep into a bale of cotton.
> But when John Henry pulled, the sun went down. And so did big John Henry!

156. Chappell, Louis W.
JOHN HENRY; A FOLK-LORE STUDY. Port Washington, N.Y., Kennikat Press [1968] 144 p. (Kennikat Press series in Negro culture and history)   PS461.J6C5 1968
Reprint of the 1933 ed.
Bibliography: p. [144]. Bibliographical footnotes.

In this study of the factual aspects of the John Henry tradition, the author examines earlier investigations, theories, the identity of John Henry, the John Henry/John Hardy confusion, the ballads, and the connection of John Henry with Big Bend Tunnel in West Virginia. An appendix supplies texts for the John Henry and John Hardy ballads.

157. Christensen, Abigail M. H.
AFRO-AMERICAN FOLK LORE; TOLD ROUND CABIN FIRES ON THE SEA ISLANDS OF SOUTH CAROLINA. New York, Negro Universities Press [1969] xiv, 116 p. illus.   PZ8.1.C462A5

A reprint of the 1892 edition retaining the earlier paternalistic preface.

The tales were told to the author by an old man whose "ol' grandaddy" had come from Africa:

> When I was a small leetle buy 'e ben hery ol', too ol' for work, an' I use for hab it for my tarsk for min'um. So 'e tell me heap o' dese story, ef I only could 'member um, dat 'e use to yeardy way ober in Arfrica.

Most of the stories are about Brer Rabbit, the "mos' cunnin' man dat go on four leg," and the manner in which he outwits Brer Wolf (though "de Wolf, 'e bery wise man") and other animals in the wood. The collection contains also another type of story often found in Africa, that of a woman who marries a tiger disguised as a man:

> An' dey went 'way down in de swamp where de Tiger hab lib, an' 'e put her dere an' tell her to stay dere tel him come back, an' dere was nuttin' for her to eat in de worl'. An' 'e lef' her all alone wid a fly to min' her. An' ef anybody trubble dat lady de fly mus' go wherebber he is an' tell um. An' dere she stayed t'ree days. Nuttin' she had to eat, nuttin' she had to look on but ole carcass an' ol' bone de Tiger done leabe dere befo'.
>
> From "De Tiger an' de Nyung Lady"

158. Cobb, Lucy M., *and* Mary A. Hicks.
ANIMAL TALES FROM THE OLD NORTH STATE. Illustrated by Inez Hogan. New York, E. P. Dutton, 1938. 200 p.
PZ8.1.C626 An

Gentle, humorous, animal stories told to the editors by "seven storytellers who have never read any of Joel Chandler Harris's animal tales." They are arranged in seven chapters, each with a different setting and a different storyteller, and always the audience is composed of white children, listening, for example, to Aunt Milly telling tales as she bakes pies. The stories are about Brer Fox, Brer Rabbit, Brer Bullfrog, Brer Goat, Brer Mockingbird, Brer Woodpecker, and other comrades. Some of the narratives, like "Where Brer Camel Got His Hump," are in the vein of the how and why story with the flavor of a proverb at the ending:

> Brer Camel am out ob de orchard to, but he has allus had er hump on his back since dat time.
> Dat am de way de worl' wags, too: one man is allus tellin' on de other ones, but den he gits ketched too, so what am de diff'rence?

One or two of the tales, such as "The Wind Spirit," suggest the American Indian.

Inez Hogan's drawings amplify the gaiety of the tales.

159. Dorson, Richard M., *comp.*
AMERICAN NEGRO FOLKTALES. Greenwich, Conn., Fawcett Publications [1967] 378, [6] p. (A Fawcett premier book, t357) GR103.D58

Bibliography: p. [379]–[381]

A volume derived from the author's two previous books of Negro oral narratives: *Negro Folktales in Michigan* (Cambridge, Harvard University Press, 1956. 245 p. GR103.D6) and *Negro Tales From Pine Bluff, Arkansas, and Calvin, Michigan* (Bloomington, Indiana University Press, 1958. 292 p. GR108.D6). From the former almost all of the tales are reprinted and from the latter more than half the contents.

In his prefatory remarks the distinguished folklorist notes that others of the tales have appeared earlier in folklore journals and that he has rearranged some of the material, brought notes up to date, and provided a new introduction.

In part 1 the author discusses at length black American folklore, its origins, its collectors, geographical distribution, and relationship to other New World folklore. He concludes:

". . . the New World Negro repertoire falls into two groups of stories, one pointing toward Africa and one pointing toward Europe and Anglo-America. The Atlantic and Caribbean islands and northeastern South America comprise the first block and the plantation states of the Old South the second block. But both story stocks draw from multiple sources." Dorson also comments on Bahamian stock figures and "the changing character" of the black folktale in this country. A detailed description of both the storytellers from whom he got the tales and their communities follows.

Part 2 contains the tales, grouped under 15 headings: Animal and Bird Stories, Old Marster and John, Colored Man and White Man, Hoodoos and Two-Heads, Spirits and Hants, Witches and Mermaids, The Lord and the Devil, Wonders, Horrors, Protest Tales, Scare Tales, Fool Tales, Lying Tales, Preachers, and Irishmen. Each of these categories has an introduction. Notes for the narratives indicate motifs, tale types, variants, and other details.

An index of motifs and tale types is appended.

160. Fauset, Arthur H.
NEGRO FOLK TALES FROM THE SOUTH (ALABAMA, MISSISSIPPI, LOUISIANA). Journal of American folk-lore, v. 40, July/Sept. 1927: 213–303.   GR1.J8, v. 40

Animal Tales, Fairy Tales, Stories of Exaggeration, Old Marster Stories, Pat and Mike, the Jew, the Negro, Riddles, Toasts, Spirituals, and Play Songs from Alabama, Louisiana, and Mississippi, collected by the author in 1925.

Popular motifs include the trickster and a dupe in the cow's belly, the Tar Baby, Rabbit in the well, and stealing the butter by playing godfather. A few of the characters are Rabbit and Fox, "Bookee" and "La Pain" (Lapin). Among the *Märchen* are variants of "Catskin," "King John and the Abbot" ("The Three Questions" here, in which an Irishman rescues a "colored man" by answering the king's questions), and "The Bremen Town Musicians" ("The Homeless Animals"). A dilemma tale, "The Three Suitors" (with a variant), appears among Stories of Exaggeration.

For the scholar and reteller.

161. Fortier, Alcée.
LOUISIANA FOLK-TALES, IN FRENCH DIALECT AND ENGLISH TRANSLATION. Boston, Published for the American Folk-

Lore Society, by Houghton, Mifflin, 1895. 122 p.
(Memoirs of the American Folk-Lore Society, v. 2)
GR1.A5, v. 2

In his introductory statement the author comments on the difficulties in making "a complete collection of the negro tales." He speaks of the origins of the tales and of their various genres—animal stories, *Märchen,* tales and songs and real *vaudevilles,* "where the song is more important than the plot"—and analyzes the Creole dialect.

The animal tales and *Märchen* have been presented here "in a faithful but not literal translation." Many of them are about stupid, greedy Compair Bouki and cunning Compair Lapin (Bouqui and Malice of Haiti, Hare and Hyena in Africa). They include "The Elephant and the Whale," in which Lapin tricks the two beasts into a tug of war, and "Compair Lapin's Godchild," in which Lapin steals Bouqui's barrel of butter (a tale comparable to the Grimms' "The Cat and Mouse in Partnership"). It ends:

> He [Bouki] looked into his barrel, there was nothing in it. Lapin had eaten all the butter.
> "Oh! that is too much," said Bouki; "he will pay me for that." He caught Lapin, he tied him with a rope, and said: "Now, what am I going to do with you? I'll throw you in the river."
> "Ah! yes, that is what I like."
> "No, you are too glad; I'll throw you in the fire."
> "Ah! yes, throw me in the fire."
> "No, you are too glad; I'll throw you in the briers."
> "Oh! I pray you, my dear Bouki, do not throw me in the briers." "Yes, it is there you must go."
> Bouki threw Lapin in the briers. As soon as he fell, he cut the rope with his teeth, and ran away, crying: "Thank you, my good Bouki; you placed me exactly where my mother resides."

The appendix presents 14 additional tales including a lengthy Tar Baby story, "Piti Bonhomme Godron"; "Grease," about a girl made of lard (forms of this occur in Africa); and "The Talking Eggs," a good child/bad child story.

162. Harris, Joel Chandler.
THE COMPLETE TALES OF UNCLE REMUS. Compiled by Richard Chase. With illustrations by Arthur Burdette Frost [and others] Boston, Houghton Mifflin, 1955. xxxii, 875 p. PZ7.H242 Co

Arranged in order of publication are the tales from *Uncle Remus: His Songs and Sayings; Nights with Uncle Remus: Myths and Legends of the Old Plantation; Daddy Jake the Runaway; and Short Stories Told After Dark; Uncle Remus and His Friends: Old Plantation Stories, Songs, and Ballads with Sketches of Negro Character; Told by Uncle Remus: New Stories of the Old Plantation; Uncle Remus and Brer Rabbit; Uncle Remus and the Little Boy; Uncle Remus Returns;* and *Seven Tales of Uncle Remus*. The original introductory material for some of the collections is included.

Richard Chase, a well-known folklorist, comments briefly on the difficulty of establishing the origin of the tales, some being a part of the folklore tradition of the Old World. He notes that the Tar Baby story appears to be African and concludes by saying: "The tales . . . have been left as Mr. Harris wrote them. Our concern has been with folktales only, and not with the songs, rhymed versions of the tales, proverbs, and character sketches. . . . Nothing has been added except a few notes on word meanings." In addition to the stories told by Uncle Remus, the editor has included one other, "Mr. Coon and the Frogs," which was told by Crazy Sue in *Daddy Jake the Runaway*.

Most of the original illustrations—by A. B. Frost, Frederick Church, J. M. Condé, E. W. Kemble, and W. H. Beard—accompany the texts.

163. ———.
NIGHTS WITH UNCLE REMUS; MYTHS AND LEGENDS OF THE OLD PLANTATION. 22d ed. Boston, Houghton Mifflin [c1883] xxxvi, 416 p. illus., plates   PZ3.H242 N 2

Of the tales in this collection the author writes: "It is safe to say, however, that the best and most characteristic of legends current on the rice plantations and Sea Islands, are also current on the cotton plantations." He discusses the "difficulty of verifying the legends, which came to hand from various sources . . . some . . . known only to the negroes who have the gift of story-telling." He points out further a relationship between a number of the characters in these stories, Brother Rabbit, for example, and Hlakanyana of the Xhosa (see "The Story of Hlakanyana" in Theal's *Kaffir Folk-Lore* (item 82), and discusses "curious parallels" within the stories to those in the Theal collection and Bleek's *Reynard the Fox* (item 163). There is, in addition, he comments, a curious likeness to certain tales among the Indians of North and

Studies and Collections for Adults

Illustration by Frost from The Complete Tales of Uncle Remus. *Item 162.*

South America. He includes a dialect vocabulary (of Daddy Jack and the Negroes on the Sea Islands) and a reprint of a French story with creole Negro dialect.

164. ———.
   UNCLE REMUS, HIS SONGS AND SAYINGS. New and rev. ed., with one hundred and twelve illustrations by A. B. Frost. New York, Appleton-Century Co., 1934. xxi, 265 p. plates.   PZ7.H242 Un 33

An edition originally published in 1903.

In his introduction the author states, "With respect to the Folk-Lore series, my purpose has been to preserve the legends themselves in their original simplicity, and to wed them permanently to the quaint dialect—if, indeed, it can be called a dialect—through the medium of which they have become a part of the domestic history of every Southern family; and I have endeavored to give to the whole a genuine flavor of the old plantation." He then proceeds to discuss his choice of variants, the songs, and the dialect itself.

Among old favorites found here are "The Wonderful Tar-

Illustration by Frost from The Complete Tales of Uncle Remus. *Item 162.*

Baby Story," "Old Mr. Rabbit, He's a Good Fisherman," and "Mr. Rabbit Nibbles Up the Butter."

165. Haywood, Charles.
 A BIBLIOGRAPHY OF NORTH AMERICAN FOLKLORE AND FOLK-SONG. 2d rev. ed. New York, Dover Publications [1961] 2 v. (xxx, 1301 p.) maps (on lining papers)
 Z5984.U5H32

Contents: v. 1. The American people north of Mexico, including Canada.—v. 2. The American Indians north of Mexico, including the Eskimos.

" . . . a compendium of our vast traditional heritage in lore and song." Entries for Book One are arranged alphabetically according to regions, ethnic backgrounds, occupations, and miscellaneous (American Characters, Our Wars—From '76 to World War II, The Shakers, and White Spirituals). Each section contains such headings as Studies and Collections, Myths—Legends, Folktales, Proverbs—Riddles, and Folksong.

The materials cited include studies, collections of tales, articles, and folk tales published in folklore and, occasionally, anthropological journals. Works published after the 1940's are not listed.

Pages 430–482 cover works about the Negro in the United States; pages 544–560, works dealing with the French-speaking Negro in the South and the Negro in the West Indies (these last are "selected"). Among the collections of tales cited, a few are for children, although these generally are not identified.

166. Hughes, Langston, *and* Arna W. Bontemps, *eds.*
THE BOOK OF NEGRO FOLKLORE. New York, Dodd, Mead, 1958. 624 p. illus. GR103.H74

In his introduction, Arna Bontemps, writer and scholar, examines Negro lore and describes its variety: animal tales with their stock characters—African prototypes and Brer Rabbit; stories of human tricksters—John/Jack against Ole Master or Old Miss; stories of exaggeration or "lies," including humorous, wry how and why stories; and preacher tales. All of these the editors represent in this rich compendium. Among other genres included are spirituals, gospel songs, rhymes, ballads (John Henry and others), the Blues, work songs, street cries, games, and playsongs.

167. Hurston, Zora N.
MULES AND MEN. With an introduction by Franz Boas. 10 illustrations by Miguel Covarrubias. New York, Negro Universities Press [1969] 342 p. GR103.H8 1969

Reprint of the 1935 ed.

Enmeshed in a running account of collecting black folklore

are tales, songs, and sermons gathered by the author, a student of anthropology, in her native Florida. The tales, narrated in heavy dialect, are most often untitled in the text but may be located by a title in the contents.

" . . . one of the few books that set black folktales in their social environment and show their social and political functions" (Julius Lester, *Black Folktales*, p. 158. See item 188).

168. Jackson, Bruce, *ed.*
FOLKLORE & SOCIETY; ESSAYS IN HONOR OF BENJ. A. BOTKIN. Hatboro, Pa., Folklore Associates, 1966. 192 p. port. GR70.J3

Includes unacc. melodies.

Bibliographical references.

In the essay "John Henry," MacEdward Leach states that the John Henry story complex "falls into three divisions: Work songs, specifically hammer songs; Ballads of John Henry; The Legend of John Henry." He describes each and their interrelationship, remarking that the legend is "based on an assortment of work songs, ballads, casual references, folk tales, and deliberate conscious invention." Thus John Henry evolves from a folk hero into a popular hero, a symbol of his people, "supreme in valor, strength, love, the conqueror of the white man's machine."

Leach examines early investigations into the genesis of the "John Henry Story complex," and the confusing of John Henry with John Hardy, black and also a steel-driver, who was hanged for killing another black while gambling. He cites references to John Henry in Jamaican songs, although there appear to be no ballads or tales with him as the central figure. However, the name is recognized: " 'John Henrdy [sic], he was a man killed on makin' dis road; de rocks mash him up.' " He concludes that the Jamaican material must be taken into account in the study of the origins of the John Henry songs and legend since the Jamaican songs provide the "oldest objective data concerning John Henry . . . older than any in the United States by at least ten years."

169. Jackson, Miles M.
A BIBLIOGRAPHY OF NEGRO HISTORY & CULTURE FOR YOUNG READERS [by] Miles M. Jackson, Jr.; assisted by Mary W. Cleaves and Alma L. Gray. [Pittsburgh] Published for

Atlanta University by the University of Pittsburgh Press [1969, c1968] xxxi, 134 p.   Z1361.N39J3

A selected, graded, annotated listing described by storyteller Spencer G. Shaw, who was consultant, Library Service to Children, Nassau Library System, Garden City, N.Y., as "another link in the communication network so essential to help destroy the invisible walls created to separate the worlds of white and Negro children." One section, Customs and Folklore, cites a small number of collections of folktales. Three works directed to adults are included because they have appeal for young readers and high school students.

170. Jagendorf, Moritz A.
    FOLK STORIES OF THE SOUTH. Illustrated by Michael Parks. New York, Vanguard Press [1972] 355 p.
                                                         GR108.J33 1972

Gathered by a folklorist and adapter of folk tales for children and arranged by state, the tales come from Alabama, Arkansas, Florida, Georgia, Louisiana, Mississippi, North Carolina, South Carolina, Tennessee, Texas, and Virginia. The stories range from the Revolution to the Civil War, from Annie Christmas to Blackbeard and a number of ghosts. In "Hoozah for Fearless Ladies and Fearless Deeds" is the story of Mammy Kate, who rescued her master when he was a British prisoner during the Revolution. "Tar-Wolf Tale" is a variant of the familiar Tar Baby story.

Among stories akin to the tall tale is one about Railroad Bill, who was "black as ebony and strong as Samson of the Bible." Another tells of Daddy Mention, a "natchral man . . . every bit as strong as John Henry . . . [who] could drive a ten-pound hammer better than a machine. And he was wiser by three thousand miles." "The Great Conjure-Alligator Man of Florida" expresses the black's intense yearning for freedom:

> Long ago there was a great conjure man in Africa. He was a good conjure man and he also was a good friend to animals, most of all to alligators, and he could change himself into one whenever he wanted to. He said the alligators were his brothers.
> One day slave traders caught him like an animal and brought him to our land to be a slave. He was sold to a master in Carolina. But he wasn't the kind to be a slave.

Notes (p. [321]–355) provide some background.

171. Johnson, Guy B.
 JOHN HENRY; TRACKING DOWN A NEGRO LEGEND. New York, AMS Press [1969] 155 p. facsim. PS461.J6J6 1969

Reprint of the 1929 ed.

Includes music.

Bibliography: p. [152]–155.

In his study of the John Henry tradition the writer examines the Big Bend Tunnel problem, John Henry's identity, the John Henry/John Hardy relationship, hammer songs, ballads, and, lastly, John Henry as a hero. He concludes: "Maybe there was no John Henry. One can easily doubt it. But there is a vivid, fascinating, tragic legend about him which Negro folk have kept alive and have cherished for more than half a century."

172. Jones, Charles C.
 NEGRO MYTHS FROM THE GEORGIA COAST, TOLD IN THE VERNACULAR. Boston, Houghton, Mifflin, 1888. Detroit, Singing Tree Press, 1969. 171 p. GR103.J6 1969

This collection of animal tales was gathered in "the swamp-region of Georgia and the Carolinas, where the lingo of the rice-field and the sea-island negroes is *sui generis,* and where myths and fanciful stories, often repeated before the war, and now seldom heard . . . materially differ from those narrated . . . in the interior." Some, like "Buh Alligatur an Buh Mash-Hen," are how and why stories. This one explains why "Buh Alligatur nebber does trubble Buh Mash-hen an eh chillun." Others point morals: "Buh Fowl-Hawk and Buh Turkey Buzzard," (" 'De man wuh trus in ehself,' moralized Daddy Sandy, 'guine fail; wile dem dat wait topper de Lord will hab perwision mek fur um,' ") and "Buh Wolf an de Two Dinner" ("People wuh wunt mek up dem mine in time wuh dem mean fuh do guine get leff.").

Includes glossary.

173. Odum, Howard W., *and* Guy B. Johnson.
 NEGRO WORKADAY SONGS. New York, Negro Universities Press [1969] 278 p. illus., music. (The University of North Carolina. Social study series)
 ML3556.O32 1969

Reprint of the 1926 ed.

Bibliography: p. [265]–270.

Here in chapter 13, "John Henry: Epic of the Negro Workingman," the John Henry ballad is described as "a rare creation of considerable originality, dignity and interest." The authors call attention to many versions of the story, all with the central theme—"John Henry, powerful steel-driving man, races with the steam-drill and dies with the hammer in his hand"—and present more than a dozen forms of the song "with some comparative evidence of the workingman's varied mirror of his hero."

174. Owen, Mary A.
VOODOO TALES, AS TOLD AMONG THE NEGROES OF THE SOUTHWEST. Collected from original sources. Introduction by Charles Godfrey Leland. Illustrated by Juliette A. Owen and Louis Wain. New York, G. P. Putnam's Sons, 1893. xv, 310 p. GR103.O8

Published in London the same year as *Old Rabbit, the Voodoo, and Other Sorcerers.*

A "very remarkable collection," notes Charles Godfrey Leland in his introduction. He continues: "There is in Missouri, as 'all along the Border,' a mixed race of Negro and Indian descent, who have inherited a vast stock of the traditions of both races, and combined or blended them strangely into new life. . . . The *stories*, in fact, all agree almost to identify with those found in the collections of Schoolcraft . . . and many others. But in the vast amount of sorcery, magic, medicine, and fetishes recorded, we find the African Voodoo ideas very strangely mixed with the *Indian*." He comments on voodooism, the lore of the woodpecker and bee (the latter he relates to Norse and Finnish beliefs), and the Negro-English speech in which the tales are told.

The lore is spun within a narrative framework which has the white child, Tow Head, visiting storytelling "old Aunties." Among the stories heard is one about the Bee-King. It begins:

> In de good ole times w'en de trees an' de beasts wuzn't feard ter talk foh fear o' bein' sot ter work, dey use ter be a heap o' spressifyin' (expressing opinions) in de woods. Special dat wuz de way mungst de bee-trees, kase (because) dey wuz feelin' mighty sweet an' peart wid dey eensides all fill up wid honey in de comb. De trees wid honey in dey hollers wuz all sot up . . . Dat's de way dey wuz. Dey wuz thes (just) dat high in dey tops dat day mos' fegit dey use ter be nuttin but saplin's a-switchin' in

de wind, an' atter dat ole holler logs twell de old king ob de bees. . . .

Characters elsewhere include witches, snakes, birds, Indian maids, and young warriors. A number of tales center on Woodpecker ("dem woodpeckeh man . . . de *rouge-nain—* de *petit homme rouge*"), who was a great sorcerer.

As in the case of Harris' stories of Brer Rabbit, the pace of these narratives is interrupted by extraneous dialog and activity on part of either Tow Head or the "old Aunties."

The book has been reissued by two publishers: in 1969 by Negro Universities Press of New York and in 1971 by Books for Libraries Press in Freeport, N.Y., as part of their Black Heritage Library Collection.

175. Parsons, Elsie W. C.
FOLK-LORE FROM THE CAPE VERDE ISLANDS. Cambridge, Mass., American Folk-Lore Society, 1923. 2 v. (Memoirs of The American Folk-Lore Society, v. 15, pt. 1–2).
GR1.A5, v. 15, pt. 1–2

Bibliography and abbreviations: p. xvii–xxv.

Tales and riddles taken down by the author from Portuguese immigrants in New England during the summers of 1916 and 1917 with assistance, in the recording, of Gregorio Teixeira da Silva.

In her preface Mrs. Parsons describes the people, their lifestyle and language, noting the formula beginnings and endings of their stories. She comments on the relationship of the tales to others, noting that most of them are akin to the European (though some are only European "in substance"), others to the African, and three (nos. 8, 53, and 63) to the tales told among the Apache, Muskhogean, and Malecite Indians.

The folktales, many with variants following, appear in English in part 1 of this two-volume work; part 2 presents the tales in the Portuguese [Negro] dialect, as well as proverbs, sayings, and riddles. The footnotes in part 1 indicating variants, parallels, and other details point up the similarities of some of the stories, such as "In the Cow's Belly," to others told in West Africa and elsewhere. Among familiar ingredients are the good child and bad child, the tug of war, the riding horse, the password, and the Tar Baby. In a trickster "cycle" of tales about Wolf (Lob'), who is greedy and stupid, and his cunning Nephew (Tobinh'), which resembles those told about Boukee and Rabbit in the Bahamas, a tale entitled "Tar Baby" begins:

> There was a wolf with a nephew. They worked on the land together. When the crops were ripe, Nephew found something stolen from the land each day. Nephew said, "I believe it's you stealing there, my Uncle Wolf." Uncle Wolf said to him, "No, it's not me, it's other people." Sir Wolf stole, stole, until almost everything was gone from the land. Nephew went to see a *saib'*; he asked him, "How can I catch my Uncle Wolf?"—"Make a figure of tar, put it in the middle of the land." Next day Uncle Wolf came, he met the tar figure.

Among the European-rooted stories is "Big-John and Little-John," a descendant of Andersen's "Big Claus and Little Claus," and, from the Grimms, "The Shoes That Were Danced to Pieces," which appears here under the same title:

> There was a king who had a daughter. The girl wore out seven pairs of shoes every night. The king announced that whoever was able to find out how she wore out her shoes might marry her and receive half of his kingdom as well; but if he tried and failed, he would have to die. Many made the attempt, but none succeeded.

The story ends with the *l'envoi*—"Little shoes run to a brook. Who is jealous, tell something better."

176. ———.
FOLK-LORE OF THE SEA ISLANDS, SOUTH CAROLINA. Foreword by Jean-Louis Brindamour. Chicago, Afro-Am Press, 1969. xxx, 216 p. GR110.S6P3 1969

Reprint of the 1923 ed.

Bibliography: p. xxvii–xxx.

Tales, riddles, and "unsophisticated beliefs" collected by the author from Sea Islanders in 1919. She prefaces her study by talking about the Islanders, their way of life and background and ties with other cultures, their store of riddles (a category including tales), the tales, narrators, local language, and collecting.

Many of the stories resemble those told in Africa, western Europe, the West Indies, and other parts of the Americas and deal with such common ingredients as playing godfather, selling mothers, guessing a name, the forbidden room, relay race, and deserted children. Brer Rabbit, Brer Fox, and Brer Wolf appear in many stories, and there are variants of the Tar Baby and Cinderella stories, Big Claus and Little Claus

("Big-Claw and Little-Claw"), and "Rumplestiltskin" ("Ramstampeldam"). This last begins:

> She was to marry to a king. An' de king said he would marry to her if she would spin a large room full of gold. An' while she was settin' down cryin',—she knew she couldn' do it,—a dwarf came an' put in an appearance.

and ends:

> So when de man came in dat day before de crowd an' deman' de chil', de queen said, "Ain't your name John? Ain't your name Peter? Ain't it Ramstampeldam?" Den de ol' man got so mad, he stamped his foot, went t'rough de floor, pop his laig off, and ran off wid one laig.

The volume also includes the sections Riddles and Proverbs, Toasts and Other Verses, Game-Songs and Other Songs, and Folk Ways and Notions.

177. Porter, Dorothy B.
   THE NEGRO IN THE UNITED STATES; A SELECTED BIBLIOGRAPHY. Washington, Library of Congress; [for sale by the Supt. of Docs., U.S. Gov't Print. Off.] 1970. 313 p.
   Z1361.N39P59

A general work in which Folk-lore and Folk-tales (p. 110–116) cites books directed to children and young people. The compiler states, however, that she made no systematic effort to represent such material, and she has not identified it as such.

178. Sale, John B.
   THE TREE NAMED JOHN. With twenty-two silhouettes by Joseph Cranston Jones. Chapel Hill, University of North Carolina Press, 1929. 151 p.
   GR103.S3

Tales, superstitions, and beliefs are interwoven in a long narrative depicting plantation life and the relationship of a white child to the blacks around him. Among the stories directly akin to those of Africa are two about Brer Rabbit told by Aunt Betsey to young John: one (p. 44–52) reveals how Brer Rabbit tricked "Brer Li-yon" into falling to his death in a well; another (p. 33–37) tells how Brer Rabbit got pop-eyes:

> Brer Rabbit allus wuz smart, he sho wuz, en eve'ybody gi'n it out, dey did, dat he wuz de smartes' somebody whut live in de woods. But Brer Rabbit wa'n't satterfied; he

kep' wantin' mo' sense. . . . Well, he worrit 'bout hit, he did, twel fus' en las', he went t' de kang uv de animals (some folks say hit 'uz a witch, en some say hit 'uz Gawd—Ah don' know 'bout dat), en he ax 'im, he did, t' git him some mo' sense. De kang said he'd do it, but fus' Brer Rabbit had t' fetch 'im a mess uv green peas f'um out'n Mist' Man's gyarden.

Brer Rabbit accomplished the three tasks, the last was to bring the king "de pizen teethes f'um Brer Rattlesnake."

W'en de kang seen him wid dem teethes, he say, "Brer Rabbit," he sez, "dar ain' no nuse uv you axin' fer no mo' sense; Ah jes ain' gwine gi' you no mo, 'ca'se you is got too much already." W'en he say dat, Brer Rabbit, he try to ack uppity, he did, en 'gun to sass him, en de kang got mad, he did, en grab 'im roun' de nake en choke 'im twel his eyes pop out jes lak you see 'em now, and dey is been dattaway ever sence.

Other animals appearing in the tales include Brer Mole, Brer Frawg, Brer Elefunt, Brer Cricket and Brer Flea. Some of the stories are untitled. Interpolated conversations often disrupt the flow of the narrative.

179. Stoney, Samuel G., *and* Gertrude M. Shelby.
BLACK GENESIS; A CHRONICLE. Illustrations by Martha Bensley Bruére. New York, Macmillan Co., 1930. xxix, 192 p.   GR103.S8

In "The Family Tree of Gullah Folk Speech and Folk Tales," which introduces this collection of Biblical and animal stories, the authors discuss the history of the Gullah dialect: "The branches of the family tree of Gullah are American, the trunk is West Indian and the roots English and African." They comment on the blacks, their coming to the West Indies and Carolina coast perhaps from Angola ("the first point of contact between negro Africa and modern Europeans") or western Liberia, on the African survivals in Gullah, and the folktales.

Arranged into 11 books, the tales are given in a modified Gullah without loss of the rhythm or the "magnificent verbiage" of the original. There are stories of the creation, of Adam and Eve, and Cain and Abel. Interwoven with these are how and why stories explaining, among other matters, the horniness of Br' Gator's hide and the short temper of Br' Wasp. Br' Rabbit is present with his customary guile. "Br'

Illustration by Frost from The Complete Tales of Uncle Remus. *Item 162.*

Rabbit Hanker for a Long Tail" reveals ties to Anansi of West Africa and Annancy of Jamaica. In this story Br' Rabbit "cock he hat an' . . . tek de path for gone to Hebben, for ax God if he won't be so kind as to gi' him a long tail like dem turrah creeter is got." And God gives him three tasks:

> "Tek dis bag, an' bring it back to me full o' black bird. . . . Knock out Br' Alligator's eye-toot's wid dis hammers, an' fetch 'em to me. . . .
> Dis-here is to fill wid Br' Deer's eye-water. You understand? Now, you git 'way from here. An' don't you come back bodderin' me till you done all de whole lot." Den he turn roun' on he heel, an' gone back in de house, an' slam de door.

180. Waterman, Richard A., *and* William R. Bascom.
AFRICAN AND NEW WORLD NEGRO FOLKLORE. *In* Funk & Wagnalls standard dictionary of folklore, mythology, and legend. v. 1. New York, Funk & Wagnalls [1949] p. 18–24.   GR35.F8, v. 1

In a survey two scholars examine the great wealth of Negro folklore and its "wide distribution and . . . remarkable toughness. . . . Surviving the drastic social changes that accompanied the forceful transplanting of African peoples into slavery on a strange continent, . . . [it] has persisted in the New World as a well-defined and basically homogeneous entity regardless of the folklore, culture, and language of the dominant groups, whether English, French, Spanish, Portuguese, Dutch, or American."

They discuss such different genres as myths, legends, folk tales or *Märchen,* proverbs, riddles, songs, and their social usage. Attention is given to the animal trickster tale, with the comment that because of the popularity of the Brer Rabbit stories, these "have come to be regarded as the typical Negro folktale." They point out the existence of human-trickster and divine-trickster tales. In their look at the trickster stories, they give examples of characteristic incidents, i.e., the trickster's contrived illness "in order to ride a powerful and important animal as if it were his horse," and point out the distinctive nature of the African trickster. Other types of tales, among these the dilemma or unfinished story, stories of ogres, of the "metamorphosed wife or husband," of food-producing pots, are described briefly.

181. Work, Monroe N.
A BIBLIOGRAPHY OF THE NEGRO IN AFRICA AND AMERICA. New York, Argosy-Antiquarian, 1965. xxi, 698 p.
Z5118.N4W6 1965
Reprint of the 1928 ed.

In his introduction Anson Phelps Stokes describes the volume as "a select reference bibliography on the Negro with more than 17,000 entries covering the most worth-while publications in different languages issued in 1928." It includes three chapters on folklore—African Folklore, Folklore of the Negro in the United States, and Folklore of the Negro in the West Indies and Latin America—containing entries selected to indicate the nature and extent of the folklore and to offer bases for comparison.

182. Writers' Program. *North Carolina.*
BUNDLE OF TROUBLES AND OTHER TARHEEL TALES, by workers of the Writers' Program of the Work Projects Administration in the State of North Carolina, edited by W. C. Hendricks; illustrations by Hilda Ogburn. Durham, N.C., Duke University Press, 1943. 206 p. plates.
(Duke University publications) GR110.N8W7

Among these tales recorded from "farmers, elderly porchwhittlers, housewives, Negro men and women, merchants, and many others" is "John Henry of Cape Fear," told by Glasgow McLeod, who claimed he knew where John Henry was born, worked with John Henry on the Santa Fe, and witnessed the contest between John Henry and the steam hammer. This account has the quality of legend:

> It was 'bout the last of May and mighty hot. John Henry was born in the fireplace room 'bout two hours atter dinner. Jes afore he was born, they come a black cloud outen the sout'west. . . .
> When John Henry was born, two men help the granny woman lift him and carry him to the tub for the wash. Then they lift that baby, what looked like a half-growed boy, and laid him on the bed, 'longside his mammy. When they laid him on the bed a big clap of lightnin' flashed clean across the sky, and the thunder, jes like a hammer, big as a barn, done hit the earth. . . .
> The storm kept gettin wurser. . . . Uncle George jumped up from his knees, where he'd been prayin', and he shouted: "Praise God, a great youngun's been borned."

In this version John Henry is a good church-going man who was "give up to be the strongest man what ever lived—stronger even than Samson, or Goliath, or ennybody." There are no references to any songs or ballads, or even Polly Ann.

Notes describing the informants are appended.

183. Writers' Program. *South Carolina*.
SOUTH CAROLINA FOLK TALES; STORIES OF ANIMALS AND SUPERNATURAL BEINGS, compiled by workers of the Writers' Program of the Work Projects Administration in the State of South Carolina. Sponsored by the University of South Carolina. Columbia, S.C. [1941] 122 p. (Bulletin of the University of South Carolina, October 1941)
GR110.S6W7

"Bibliography for South Carolina folk tales": p. 118–122.

Animal stories and stories of the supernatural selected from "several thousand manuscripts assembled . . . between 1935 and 1941." In her preface Mabel Montgomery, state supervisor, writes that "a large part of the collection was secured from Negroes on the coast and barrier islands of the State." She describes the geographical area, the local speech, and efforts of project workers to render the tales in a form outsiders could read.

Studies and Collections for Adults 145

From John Henry and the Double
Jointed Steam-Drill *by Irwin Shapiro,
illustrated by James Daugherty. Item 190.*

The stories, in two main sections, each with an introduction, are told in a straightforward manner and accompanied by comparative notes. The supernatural stories are preceded by a list and description of such beings as "boo-daddies," drolls, and "plat-eyes." A number of the animal stories have elements popular in Africa and in the West Indies. One of these is "Three Tasks" (p. 17):

> Bruh Rabbit went to cote King daughtah en King tell um: "If you go to wuk en ketch deer en git eye watah outa deer eye, you kin marry muh daughtah."

> Bruh Rabbit went out wid half-hitch ob rope een 'e han en meet Bruh Deer.
> 'E seh, "Bruh Deer, O, Bruh Deer, bet you can' put yo haid tru dis rope."
> Bruh Deer seh 'e bet 'e kin, so 'e put 'e haid een rope.
> Bruh Rabbit pull rope tight en seh, "Bruh Deer, cry—cry, Bruh Deer," en Bruh Rabbit ketch tear in bottle en carry um to King.

COLLECTIONS FOR CHILDREN

184. Cothran, Jean, comp.
THE WHANG DOODLE; FOLK TALES FROM THE CAROLINAS. Illustrated by Nance Studio. [Columbia, S.C.] Sandlapper Press [1972] 90 p.   PZ8.1.C79 Wh

A selection of tales representing three "major" groups of Carolina folk tradition, i.e., Indian, British, and black. The largest number are from the blacks. Of these "The Whang Doodle" is said to be based on an experience the narrator had as a child, but it has elements of folk imagination. She has modified the Gullah dialect of stories from the South Carolina coast, as evidenced in this piece from "The Rabbit, Fox, and Goose":

> What start the thing off? There was a man who had a garden of vegetables and a little girl. The little girl stayed home, but the father always went to work.
> Now Buddah Rabbit was tricky and cunning, so he came to the garden and called, "Lil gal! Oh lil gal!"

The source of each story is stated.
The reteller's *With a Wig, With a Wag* (New York, D. McKay [1954] PZ8.1.C79 Wi) contains two more black tales: "Mister Deer's My Riding Horse" (a retelling of one of the *Two Negro Tales*, recorded by Mrs. William Preston Johnson, *Journal of American Folk-Lore*, v. 9, 1896) and "Mister Honey Mouth" (a retelling from Alcée Fortier's *Louisiana Folk-Tales*, item 161).

185. Courlander, Harold.
TERRAPIN'S POT OF SENSE. Illustrated by Elton Fax. New York, Holt [1957] 125 p.   PZ8.1.C8 Te

The 31 stories assembled here reveal the variety and richness of the black American folk heritage. Gathered by a well-known folklorist from black storytellers in rural Alabama, New Jersey, and Michigan, they represent selections from the Buh Rabbit cycle, preacher and devil stories, tall tales ("big lies"), and plantation stories, the last revolving around the slave cultural heroes Big John, George, and Okra.

In the appended Notes on the Stories the author describes problems encountered in the transcription of the tales—dialect, style, and choice of characters, the last often a matter of local tradition or preference. He also discusses West African precedents, citing, for example, the relationship of Buh Rabbit to the spider trickster, the hare trickster, and the mouse deer of Indonesia and Malaya. Notes for the individual stories indicate variants.

Elton Fax's black-and-white drawings augment the flavor of the text.

186. Harris, Joel Chandler.
 BRER RABBIT; STORIES FROM UNCLE REMUS . . . adapted by Margaret Wise Brown, with the A. B. Frost pictures redrawn for reproduction by Victor Dowling. New York, Harper [c1941] 132 p. PZ7.H242Br

A selection of Brer Rabbit stories from *Nights With Uncle Remus, Myths and Legends of the Old Plantation* (item 163) and *Uncle Remus, His Songs and Sayings* (item 164). Margaret Wise Brown remarks in her foreword that she has omitted the original literary framework of the stories, modified the dialect employed in conversation by the animals, and removed interpolated passages, while attempting to be faithful to the rhythm of the stories.

> One day when Brer Rabbit, and Brer Fox, and Brer Coon, and Brer Bear, and a whole lot of them were clearing up a new ground for to plant a roasting-ear patch, the sun began to get sort of hot, and Brer Rabbit, he got tired; but he didn't let on, because he feared the balance of them would call him lazy. So he kept on toting off trash and piling up brush, till by-and-by he hollers out that he got a brier in his hand, and then he takes and slips off to hunt for a cool place for to rest. After a while he came across a well with a bucket hanging in it.
> "Dat look cool," sez Brer Rabbit, sezee, "en cool I 'spect she is. . . ."
> From "Old Mr. Rabbit, He's a Good Fisherman"

Illustration by Frost from The Complete Tales of Uncle Remus. Item 162.

187. ———.
THE FAVORITE UNCLE REMUS; illustrated by A. B. Frost. Selected, arranged, & edited by George Van Santvoord and Archibald C. Coolidge. [Boston] Houghton Mifflin Co., 1948. 310 p.   PZ7.H242 Fav

A selection of some of the best loved tales found in seven of Joel Chandler Harris' works: *Uncle Remus, His Songs and His Sayings* (item 164); *Nights With Uncle Remus; Myths and Legends of the Old Plantation* (item 163); *Daddy Jake the Runaway, and Short Stories Told After Dark* (New York, Century Co., 1889); *Uncle Remus and His Friends; Old Plantation Stories, Songs and Ballads, With Sketches of Negro Character* (Boston, Houghton, Mifflin, 1892); *Told by Uncle Remus; New Stories of the Old Plantation* (New York, McClure, Philips, 1905); *Uncle Remus and the Little Boy* (Boston, Small, Maynard, 1910); and *Uncle Remus Returns* (Boston, Houghton Mifflin Co., 1918). The editors have

From The Knee-High Man, and Other Tales *by Julius Lester, illustrated by Ralph Pinto. See item 188.*

removed some interpolated passages and diminished the literary setting.

A. B. Frost's famous illustrations have been retained.

188. Lester, Julius.
BLACK FOLKTALES. Illustrated by Tom Feelings. New York, Grove Press [1970, c1969] 159 p. (An Evergreen black cat book, B-262)   PZ8.1.L434B13

Twelve short stories, some of them still told in African towns and villages and others "on the street corners, stoops, porches, in bars, barber shops, and wherever else in America black people gather." The author, a well-known writer, has molded them "to his tongue and to his mouth," for stories are "living, growing, changing thing[s]." Thus these tales have a contemporary colloquial flavor.

The stories center on four topics: Origins, Love, Heroes, and People. Some are humorous, some poignant, and all evoke the emotions of oppression. In an Afterword sources are cited for 11 of the stories.

In *The Knee-High Man, and Other Tales,* with pictures by Ralph Pinto (New York, Dial Press [1972] 28 p.), Lester has taken six stories—chiefly animal tales—and retold them for younger children. For these an appendix indicates sources.

189. Love, Rose L., *ed.*
A COLLECTION OF FOLKLORE FOR CHILDREN IN ELEMENTARY SCHOOL AND AT HOME. New York, Vantage Press [1964] 83 p. illus. GR105.L6

Includes music.

Compiled by the author for use in elementary schools, this is an excellent selection of folk rhymes, stories, songs, and games. Their rendition in "correct usage to help the children who will use . . . [the book] and hear it read," however, illustrates the loss of flavor which occurs when sources are used literally without the adaptor's ear being attuned to the storyteller's natural rhythm.

Examples of tales appearing in the Uncle Remus collections (items 163, 164, 186, and 187) are: "The Well Saves Mr. Rabbit" ("Old Mr. Rabbit, He's a Good Fisherman"), "Mr. Rabbit and the Tar Baby" ("The Wonderful Tar-Baby Story"), and "Mr. Rabbit's Riding Horse" ("Mr. Rabbit Grossly Deceives Mr. Fox"):

> Mr. Fox and Mr. Rabbit both liked Miss Froggie. Mr Rabbit like to talk about Mr. Fox to Miss Froggie.
> One day, he said, "Miss Froggie, I can make Mr. Fox do anything. Sometimes he carries me on his back. He is my Riding Horse. Next time, I come to see you, I'll ride here on his back."

190. Shapiro, Irwin.
JOHN HENRY AND THE DOUBLE JOINTED STEAM-DRILL. With drawings by James Daugherty. New York, J. Messner [1945] [55] p. PS461.J6S5

A literary adaptation, told in rhythmic prose that carries the spirit of the songs in the text. Here John Henry rousts cotton, feuds with John Hardy, and becomes a steel-driving man. "John Henry drove steel every day. He traveled to almost every state of the Union, driving steel. He worked for the

B. & O. Railroad, and the C. & O. Railroad . . . and lots more." In his contest with the steam drill, John Henry won. "Talk and songs alike say he died with his hammer in his hand. . . . No such thing! Couldn't any steam drill send John Henry to his lonely grave! No, sir! Not John Henry!"

Many vigorous drawings by James Daugherty.

From Ananse the Spider: Tales from an Ashanti Village *by Peggy Appiah, illustrated by Peggy Wilson. Item 48.*

Index

Keyed to entry numbers

Aardema, Verna, 46, 47, 84, 110
Adu, Omotayo, 34
The Adventures of Spider; West African Folk Tales, 49
"African and New World Negro Folklore," 180
African Folk Tales, 12, 57, 129
African Folklore, 1
African Genesis, 11
African Mythology, 5
African Myths and Legends, 13
African Myths, Together With Proverbs; a Supplementary Reader, 18
African Proverbs, Tales and Historical Fragments, 42
The African Saga, 10
African Wonder Tales, 15
Africana: Folklore Collections for Children, 3
Afro-American Folk Lore; Told Round Cabin Fires on the Sea Islands of South Carolina, 157
Agikuyu Folk Tales, 128
Akamba Stories, 114
Akan-Ashanti Folk-Tales, 40
Alegría, Ricardo E., 145
The Alo Man; Stories From the Congo, 99
American Negro Folktales, 159
Among the Ibos of Nigeria, 20
Among the Primitive Bakongo, 98
Anancy Stories and Dialect Verse, 133

Ananse the Spider: Tales From an Ashanti Village, 48
Anansi, the Spider Man; Jamaican Folk Tales, 149
Animal Tales From the Old North State, 158
Animals Mourn for Da Leopard, and Other West African Tales, 55
Anthologie aus der Suaheli-Litteratur, 112
Appiah, Peggy, 48
Arkhurst, Joyce C., 49
Arnott, Kathleen, 13
Ashabranner, Brent, 123

Bacon, A. M., 152
The Baganda; an Account of Their Native Customs and Beliefs, 118
Bahama Songs and Stories; a Contribution to Folk-Lore, 139
Bantu Folk Tales, Seven Stories, 87
Bantu Tales, 102
Barker, William H., 19
Bascom, William R., 180
Basden, George T., 20
Baskerville, Rosetta G. H., 121
Basutoland; Its Legends and Customs, 79
Bateman, George W., 120
Baumbach, E. J. M., 65
The Bavenda, 81
Beckwith, Martha W., 134
Beech, Mervyn W. H., 104

Behind the Back of the
   Mountain; Black Folktales
   From Southern Africa, 84
Beier, Ulli, 29
Belpré, Pura, 146
Bennett, John, 153
Bennett, Louise, 133, 141
Berger, Terry, 85
Bertol, Roland, 50
Bibliography of African Oral
   Narratives, 6
A Bibliography of Negro
   History & Culture for
   Young Readers, 169
A Bibliography of North
   American Folklore and
   Folksong, 165
A Bibliography of the Negro
   in Africa and America, 181
Bishop, Herbert L., 66
Black Fairy Tales, 85
Black Folktales, 167, 188
Black Genesis; a Chronicle,
   179
Bleek, D. F., 67
Bleek, Wilhelm H. I., 1, 67-69,
   86
Blooah, Charles G., 3
Bontemps, Arna W., 165
The Book of Negro Folklore,
   166
Botkin, Benjamin A., 153
Bourhill, Mrs. E. J., 17, 85
Bowman, James C., 154
Bradford, Roark, 155
Brer Rabbit; Stories From
   Uncle Remus, 187
The Bride Who Wanted a
   Special Present, and Other
   Tales From Western Kenya,
   130
The British Folklorists; a
   History, 2
Brownlee, Frank, 70
Bryan, Ashley, 14
Büttner, Carl, 112

The Bull of the Kraal and the
   Heavenly Maidens; a Tale
   of Black Children, 88
Bundle of Troubles and
   Other Tarheel Tales, 182
Burton, William F. P., 91
The Bushmen and Their
   Stories, 86

Cagnolo, C., 105
Callaway, Canon, 1
Callaway, Henry, Bp., 71
Canu, Gaston, 21
Cardinall, Allan W., 22
Carpenter, Frances, 15
Carter, Dorothy S., 147
Cendrars, Blaise, 10
Chadwick, Mara L. P., 99
Les Chants et les contes des
   Ba-Ronga de la baie de
   Delagoa, 75
Chappell, Louis W., 156
Chase, Richard, 162
Chatelain, Héli, 72
The Children of Ananse, 48
Children of Yayoute; Folk
   Tales of Haiti, 138
Christensen, Abigail M. H.,
   157
Cobb, Lucy M., 158
Cobble, Alice D., 100
A Collection of Folklore for
   Children in Elementary
   School and at Home, 189
Collections of African Folk-
   lore for Children, 7
Comhaire-Sylvain, Suzanne,
   135
Congo Fireside Tales, 103
Congo Life and Folklore, 98
Contes mossi actuels; étude
   ethno-linguistique, 21
Contes populaires d'Afrique
   occidentale, 29
Contes populaires des Bas-
   soutos (Afrique du Sud), 74

Index

Cothran, Jean, 184
Courlander, Harold, 16, 23, 51–53, 122, 136, 148, 185
The Cow-tail Switch, and Other West African Stories, 51
Creel, J. Luke, 54
"Creole Tales From Haiti," 135
Cronise, Florence M., 24
Crowley, Daniel J., 137
Cunnie Rabbit, Mr. Spider, and the Other Beef; West African Folk Tales, 24

Daddy Jake the Runaway, and Short Stories Told After Dark, 162, 187
Dahal, Charity, 132
Dahomean Narrative; a Cross-Cultural Analysis, 32
The Dancing Palm Tree, and Other Nigerian Folktales, 64
David He No Fear, 32
Davis, Mary Gould, 126
Davis, Russell G., 123
Dayrell, Elphinstone, 25
Dennett, Richard E., 92
Des Prés, François Marcel-Turenne, 138
The Doctor to the Dead; Grotesque Legends and Folk Tales of Old Charleston, 153
Doke, Clement M., 93
Dorliae, Peter G., 55
Dorson, Richard M., 1, 2, 159
Drake, Mrs. J. B., 17, 85
The Drum and the Hoe; Life and Lore of the Haitian People, 136
Dundas, Sir Charles, 106

Edgar, Frank, 26, 36

Edwards, Charles L., 139
Ellis, Alfred B., 27
Ennis, Merlin, 28
Equilbecq, Victor François, 29
Eshugbayi, Ezekiel A., 52
The Essential Kafir, 76
Ethnology of A-Kamba and Other East African Tribes, 109
Evans-Pritchard, Sir Edward E., 107
Every Man Heart Lay Down, 32
The Ewe-Speaking Peoples of the Slave Coast of West Africa, Their Religion, Manners, Customs, Laws, Languages, etc., 27
Fairy Tales From South Africa, 17, 85
Fauset, Arthur H., 160
The Favorite Uncle Remus, 187
Finnegan, Ruth H., 30
The Fire on the Mountain, and Other Ethiopian Stories, 122
The Flame Tree and Other Folk-Lore Stories From Uganda, 121
The Fly Whisk, and Other Stories From Masailand, 132
Folk Stories From Southern Nigeria, West Africa, 25
Folk Stories of the South, 170
Folk Tales and Fables, 36
Folk Tales From Ankole, 116
Folk Tales of Liberia, 54
Folklore & Society; Essays in Honor of Benj. A. Botkin, 168
"Folk-Lore From Elizabeth City County, Virginia," 152
Folk-Lore From the Cape Verde Islands, 175

Folk-Lore of the Antilles,
    French and English, 144
Folk-Lore of the Sea Islands,
    South Carolina, 176
The Folktale, 8
Folk-Tales of Andros Island,
    Bahamas, 143
Folk-Tales of Angola, 72
Folktales of Zambia, 97
Fortier, Alcée, 161
Fourteen Hundred Cowries,
    and Other African Tales,
    56
Fox, Douglas C., 11
Frobenius, Leo, 11
Frost, A. B., 162, 187
Fuja, Abayomi, 56

Gassire's Lute, 11
Gassire's Lute; a West African
    Epic, 59
Gbadamosi, Bakare, 31
Gecau, Rose, 108
Gichuru, Stephen, 132
God Wash the World and
    Start Again, 32
Görög-Karady, Veronika, 3
Graham, Lorenz B., 32
Greedy Mariani and Other
    Folktales of the Antilles,
    147
Guillot, René, 57
Guirma, Frederic, 58
Gurrey, Percival, 36

Harman, Humphrey, 124
Harris, Joel Chandler, 162–
    164, 187
The Hat-Shaking Dance, and
    Other Tales From the Gold
    Coast, 52
Hausa Folk-lore, Customs,
    Proverbs, etc., 41
Hausa Superstitions and Cus-
    toms; an Introduction to
    the Folk-lore and the Folk,
    44

Hausa Tales and Traditions,
    26
Haywood, Charles, 165
Heady, Eleanor B., 125
Helfman, Elizabeth S., 86
Herman, Gertrude B., 3
Herskovits, Frances S., 33
Herskovits, Melville J., 33
Hertslet, Jessie, 87
Herzog, George, 34, 50
Hicks, Mary A., 158
Hobley, Charles W., 109
Holladay, Virginia, 102
Hollis, Sir Alfred C., 47, 110,
    111
Honeij, James A., 73
Hongry Catch the Foolish
    Boy, 32
How God Fix Jonah, 32
How the Donkeys Came to
    Haiti and Other Tales, 142
Hughes, Langston, 166
Hurston, Zora N., 167

I Could Talk Old-Story Good:
    Creativity in Bahamian
    Folklore, 137
Idewu, Olawale, 35
The Iguana's Tail; Crick
    Crack Stories From the
    Caribbean, 150
In the Shadow of the Bush, 43
Iremonger, Lucille, 140
Itayemi, Phebean, 36

Jablow, Alta, 59
Jabo Proverbs From Liberia;
    Maxims in the Life of a
    Native Tribe, 33
Jackson, Bruce, 168
Jackson, Miles M., 169
Jacottet, Édouard, 74
Jagendorf, Moritz A., 170
Jamaica Anansi Stories, 134
Jamaican Song and Story:
    Annancy Stories, Digging

*Sings, Ring Tunes, and
  Dancing Tunes,* 141
*Jambo, Sungura! Tales From
  East Africa,* 125
Jekyll, Walter, 141
John Henry, 155
*John Henry, a Folk-Lore
  Study,* 156
*John Henry and the Double
  Jointed Steam-Drill,* 190
*John Henry, the Rambling
  Black Ulysses,* 154
*John Henry; Tracking Down
  a Negro Legend,* 171
Johnson, Guy B., 171, 173
Johnson, Gyneth, 142
Johnston, Hugh A. S., 37
Jones, Charles C., 172
Junod, Henri A., 75

Kaffir Folk-lore, 82, 163
Kalibala, Ernest B., 126
Kamba Folklore, 113
Kiahon, Bai Gai, 54
Kidd, Dudley, 76, 77, 88
Kikuyu Folktales, 108
Kikuyu Tales, 105
*Kilimanjaro and Its People; a
  History of the Wachagga,*
  106
*The King of the Snakes and
  Other Folk-Lore Stories
  From Uganda,* 121
*The King's Drum, and Other
  African Stories,* 16
Kingsley, Mary H., 91
Knappert, Jan, 94, 112
*The Knee-High Man, and
  Other Tales,* 188
Krige, Eileen, 71
Kuguru, Peter, 132

Lamba Folk-Lore, 93
Lang, Andrew, 24
Lantum, Daniel, 101
Leland, Charles Godfrey, 174

Leshoai, Benjamin L., 89
Leslau, Charlotte, 12
Leslau, Wolf, 12, 122
Lester, Julius, 188
*The Life of a South African
  Tribe,* 75
*Limba Stories and Story-
  Telling,* 30
Lindblom, Gerhard, 113
*Lion and Jackal, With Other
  Native Folk Tales From
  South Africa,* 70
*The Lion on the Path, and
  Other African Stories,* 7, 90
*Lion Outwitted by Hare, and
  Other African Tales,* 17
*The Lion's Whiskers; Tales
  of High Africa,* 123
*Litafi na Tatsuniyoyi na
  Hausa,* 26
*Littérature orale de l'Afrique
  noire; bibliographie analy-
  tique,* 4
Lloyd, Lucy C., 67, 69
Lord, Albert B., 27
*Louisiana Folk-Tales, in
  French Dialect and English
  Translation,* 161
Love, Rose L., 189
*Lyuba; Traditional Religion
  of the Sukuma,* 115

*Märchen und Erzählungen
  der Suaheli,* 112
*Magána Hausa. Native Liter-
  ature, or Proverbs, Tales,
  Fables and Historical Frag-
  ments in the Hausa Lan-
  guage,* 42
*The Magic Drum; Tales From
  Central Africa,* 91
*The Mantis and His Friends;
  Bushman Folklore,* 67
Marivate, C. T. D., 65
Markowitz, Arthur, 78
Marsh, Gwen, 57

Martin, Minnie, 79
The Masai: Their Language and Folklore, 110
Masilo's Adventures, and Other Stories, 89
Mbata, A. H. S., 87
Mbiti, John S., 114
Mdhladhla, G. C. S., 87
Mesfin Habte-Mariam, 127
Millroth, Berta, 115
More Tales From the Story Hat, 46
Mules and Men, 167
Mushanga, Musa T., 116
My Dark Companions and Their Strange Stories, 95
The Mythical & Traditional History of Dagomba, 22
The Mythology of All Races, 9
Myths and Legends of the Bantu, 9
Myths & Legends of the Congo, 94
Myths & Legends of the Swahili, 112

The Na of Wa, 47
The Nandi: Their Language and Folk-Lore, 111
Nassau, Robert H., 38
"Negro Folk Tales From the South (Alabama, Mississippi, Louisiana)," 160
The Negro in the United States; a Selected Bibliography, 177
Negro Myths From the Georgia Coast, Told in the Vernacular, 172
Negro Workaday Songs, 173
Nettleford, Rex, 141
Niane, Djibril T., 39
Niger Ibos, 20
Nigerian Folk Tales, 35
Nights With Uncle Remus:

Myths and Legends of the Old Plantation, 162, 163, 187
Njoroge, J. K., 132
Njururi, Ngumbu, 128
Not Even God Is Ripe Enough: Yoruba Stories, 31
Notes on the Folk-Lore of the Fjort (French Congo), 92
Nunn, Jessie A., 129
Nursery Tales, Traditions, and Histories of the Zulus, in Their Own Words, 71

Odum, Howard W., 173
Okeke, Uche, 60
Olode the Hunter, and Other Tales From Nigeria, 53
Oral Literature in Africa, 30
The Orange Thieves, 132
Osogo, John N. B., 130
Otwe, 47
Owen, Mary A., 174
The Ox of the Wonderful Horns, and Other African Folktales, 14

Parrinder, Edward Geoffrey, 5
Parsons, Elsie W. C., 143, 144, 152, 175, 176
The Piece of Fire, and Other Haitian Tales, 148
The Pineapple Child, and Other Tales From Ashanti, 48
Porter, Dorothy B., 177
Postma, Minnie, 80
Prempeh, Albert Kofi, 52
Price, Christine, 127
Princess of the Full Moon, 58
The Proud Ostrich, and Other Tales, 132

Rattray, Robert S., 40, 41, 117
Reynard the Fox, 163
Reynard the Fox in South

Africa; or, Hottentot Fables and Tales, 68
The Rich Man and the Singer; Folktales From Ethiopia, 127
A Road Down in the Sea, 32
Robinson, Adjai, 61
Le Roman de Bouqui, 135
Roscoe, John, 118
Routledge, Katherine P., 119
Routledge, William S., 119

Safiri the Singer, East African Tales, 125
Sale, John B., 178
Savage Childhood; a Study of Kafir Children, 77
Savory, Phyllis, 17, 103
Scheub, Harold, 6
Schmidt, Nancy J., 7
Schön, James F., 42
A Selection of Hausa Stories, 37
A Selection of ŠiRonga Folklore, 66
Serwadda, W. Moses, 131
Seven Tales of Uncle Remus, 162
Shapiro, Irwin, 190
Shelby, Gertrude M., 179
Sherlock, *Sir* Philip M., 133, 141, 149–151
Sidahome, Joseph E., 62
Sinclair, Cecilia, 19
Singing Tales of Africa, 61
Skinner, Neil, 26
The Sky-God Stories, 47
The Social System of the Zulus, 71
Some Folk-lore Stories and Songs in Chinyanja, 117
Songs and Stories From Uganda, 131
South African Folk Tales, 73
South Carolina Folk Tales; Stories of Animals and

Supernatural Beings, 183
Specimens of Bantu Folk-Lore From Northern Rhodesia, 96
Specimens of Bushman Folklore, 69
Stanley, *Sir* Henry Morton, 95
Stayt, Hugh A., 81
Steere, Edward, 112, 120
Stoney, Samuel G., 179
Stories of the Benin Empire, 62
Sturton, Hugh, 63
The Suk; Their Language and Folklore, 104
Sundiata: an Epic of Old Mali, 39
Sundiata: the Epic of the Lion King, 50
Swahili Tales, 112
Swahili Tales, as Told by Natives of Zanzibar, 120

The Tailed Head-Hunters of Nigeria, 45
Talbot, Percy A., 43
Tales for the Third Ear, From Equatorial Africa, 47
Tales From the Basotho, 86
Tales From the Story Hat, 46
Tales of an Ashanti Father, 48
Tales of Land of Death: Igbo Folktales, 60
Tales of Mogho; African Stories From Upper Volta, 58
Tales of Nso, 101
Tales of the African Wilds, 79
The Tales of Wamugumo, 132
Tales of Yoruba Gods and Heroes, 23
Tales Told in Togoland, 22
Tales Told Near a Crocodile; Stories From Nyanza, 124
Tamakloe, E. F., 22
Tatsuniyoyi na Hausa, 26, 37

Terrapin's Pot of Sense, 185
Theal, George M., 1, 82, 83
Thompson, Stith, 8
The Three Wishes; a Collection of Puerto Rican Folktales, 145
The Tiger and the Rabbit, and Other Tales, 146
Told by Uncle Remus: New Stories of the Old Plantation, 162, 187
Torrend, J., 96
Tracey, Hugh, 7, 90
The Treasury of Ba-suto Lore; Being Original Se-suto Texts, 74
A Treasury of Southern Folklore; Stories, Ballads, Traditions and Folkways of the People of the South, 153
The Tree Named John, 178
Tremearne, Arthur J. N., 2, 44, 45
The Tshi-Speaking Peoples of the Gold Coast of West Africa; Their Religion, Manners, Customs, Laws, Languages, etc., 27

uHlabanengalwi, 87
Umbundu; Folk Tales From Angola, 28
Uncle Bouqui of Haiti, 148
Uncle Remus and Brer Rabbit, 162
Uncle Remus and His Friends: Old Plantation Stories, Songs, and Ballads With Sketches of Negro Character, 162, 187
Uncle Remus and the Little Boy, 162, 187
Uncle Remus: His Songs and Sayings, 162, 164, 187
Uncle Remus Returns, 162, 187

Velten, Carl, 112
Voodoo Tales; as Told Among the Negroes of the Southwest, 174
Vyas, Chiman L., 97

Wakaima and the Clay Man, and Other African Folktales, 126
Walker, Barbara K., 34, 64
Walker, Warren S., 34
Wamugumo, 132
Ward, Henry W., 23
Waterman, Richard A., 180
Weeks, John H., 98
Wembi, the Singer of Stories, 100
Werner, Alice, 9, 141
West African Folk-Tales, 19
West Indian Folk-Tales, 151
West Indian Folk-Tales: Anansi Stories, Tales From West Indian Folk-Lore, 140
The Whang Doodle; Folk Tales From the Carolinas, 184
When the Stones Were Soft: East African Fireside Tales, 125
Where Animals Talk; West African Folk Lore Tales, 38
"Why the Sun and the Moon Live in the Sky," 24
With a Prehistoric People: the Akikuyu of British East Africa, 119
With a Wig, With a Wag, 184
With Uplifted Tongue: Stories, Myths and Fables of the South African Bushmen, Told in Their Manner, 78
Woodson, Carter G., 18
Work, Monroe N., 181
Writers' Program. North Carolina, 182

Writers' Program.
  South Carolina, 183
Xironga Folk-tales, 65
The Yellow and Dark-Skinned
  People of Africa South of
  the Zambesi, 83
The Yoruba-Speaking Peoples of the Slave Coast of
  West Africa; Their Religion, Manners, Customs,
  Laws, Language, etc., 27

The Zande Trickster, 107
Zanzibar Tales Told by
  Natives of the East Coast
  of Africa, 120
Zomo, the Rabbit, 63